CW00431905

ISBN:9798378277377
First edition, 2023

The Power of Motivation and Innovation: Achieving Success in Today's World

Motivation and innovation are two key drivers of success in any field. As an author for over two decades, I have seen firsthand the power that these two factors can have in helping people achieve their goals and reach new heights of success. In this introduction, I will explore the importance of motivation and innovation, using examples from my own experience as well as from the world around us.

Motivation is the driving force that keeps us moving forward, even in the face of challenges and obstacles. Without motivation, it can be difficult to stay focused on our goals and push ourselves to achieve them. One example of motivation in action can be seen in the world of sports, where athletes must constantly push themselves to perform at their best. Whether it's training for a marathon or competing in the Olympics, athletes rely on their motivation to stay focused and achieve their goals.

Innovation is another crucial factor in achieving success. By constantly looking for new and better ways to do things, we can improve our processes, products, and services, and stay ahead of the competition. One example of innovation in action can be seen in the tech industry, where companies are constantly pushing the boundaries of what is possible. From smartphones to social media, these innovations have transformed the way we live and work.

Motivation and innovation are not just important for individuals and companies, but for society as a whole. By staying motivated and innovative, we can tackle some of the biggest challenges facing our world today, from climate change to social inequality. For example, many companies are now focusing on developing sustainable technologies and practices to help reduce our impact on the environment.

Of course, staying motivated and innovative is not always easy. It can be tempting to stick with what we know, or to give up when things get tough. However, by embracing a growth mindset and constantly challenging ourselves, we can keep moving forward and achieving our goals. This can be seen in the story of Elon Musk, who has overcome countless setbacks to build some of the most innovative companies of our time.

Motivation and innovation are two essential ingredients for success, both at the individual and societal level. By staying motivated and looking for new and better ways to do things, we can achieve great things and make a positive impact on the world around us. So whether you're an athlete, a business owner, or just someone looking to make a difference, remember the power of motivation and innovation, and use it to your advantage.

"You miss 100% of the shots you don't take." - Wayne Gretzky"

Brian Chesky

In 2007, Brian Chesky and Joe Gebbia were struggling to pay the rent on their San Francisco apartment. They had recently quit their jobs to start a business together, but their initial idea wasn't gaining much traction. They needed a new plan, and fast.

Around the same time, the city was preparing to host a major design conference, and all of the hotels in the area were fully booked. Chesky and Gebbia realized that there was an opportunity there: what if they rented out air mattresses in their living room to conference attendees who couldn't find a place to stay?

They quickly threw together a simple website, called it "Air Bed and Breakfast," and started promoting their idea on social media. They managed to attract a few customers, but not enough to make a real business out of it.

Still, they were encouraged by the response, and they realized that they might be onto something. They spent the next several months refining their concept, testing it with friends and family, and looking for ways to make it more appealing to potential customers.

Eventually, they came up with a new idea: what if instead of just renting out air mattresses in their own apartment, they created a platform that allowed anyone to rent out spare rooms or entire homes to travelers? They called it Airbnb, and in 2008, they launched the first version of the website.

It wasn't an immediate success, but they persisted, taking advantage of every opportunity to promote their service and improve the user experience. They traveled around the country, meeting with hosts and users, and gathering feedback to make the platform more appealing and user-friendly.

Their perseverance paid off. Today, Airbnb is one of the most valuable startups in the world, with a market capitalization of over $100 billion. Chesky and Gebbia's willingness to take a chance on a risky idea, even after their first attempt didn't work out, is a perfect example of the kind of boldness and resilience that Wayne Gretzky's famous quote encourages.

"The future belongs to those who believe in the beauty of their dreams." - Eleanor Roosevelt

Sara Blakely

In 1971, Sara Blakely came into the world in Clearwater, Florida, and later earned a degree in Communications from Florida State University. After college, she worked for a few months at Walt Disney World before taking a job selling fax machines door-to-door in the Atlanta area.

It was during her time selling office supplies that Sara had the idea for Spanx. One day, she was getting dressed for a party and realized that she didn't have the right undergarments to wear under a pair of white pants. She tried on a few pairs of pantyhose, but they all had visible lines and seams that ruined the smooth look she was going for. Frustrated, she cut the feet off a pair of pantyhose and wore them instead. This gave her the smooth silhouette she wanted, but the feet kept rolling up and creating an uncomfortable bunching effect.

That's when Sara had her "aha!" moment. She realized that footless pantyhose made from a special, stretchy fabric that smoothed out bumps and lines while still being comfortable and breathable would be a game changer for women everywhere.

Sara started working on her idea in the evenings and on weekends, while still selling fax machines during the day. She researched fabrics and manufacturers, and eventually came up with a prototype that she felt was perfect. But when she started pitching her product to hosiery manufacturers and retailers, she faced a lot of rejection. Many of them didn't see the value in a footless pantyhose, and others didn't take her seriously because she had no background in fashion or design.

Undeterred, Sara continued to believe in the beauty of her dream. She used her savings to launch a website for Spanx, and started selling her product directly to customers. She also sent free samples to fashion editors and celebrities, hoping to generate some buzz. Her big break came when she landed a meeting with the buyers at Neiman Marcus, one of the country's most prestigious department stores. They loved the product, and agreed to carry Spanx in their stores.

From there, things took off. Oprah Winfrey named Spanx one of her favorite things in 2000, and sales skyrocketed. Sara quit her job selling fax machines and devoted herself full-time to the company. She expanded the product line to include other undergarments, as well as swimwear and activewear. Today, Spanx is a global brand with a loyal following of women who swear by its shaping and smoothing products.

Sara's success is a testament to the power of believing in your dreams, even when they seem far-fetched or impossible. She had no experience in fashion, no backing from investors, and no connections in the industry, but she persevered and created a product that filled a real need for women. Her story is a reminder that with hard work, determination, and a little bit of luck, anything is possible.

"Success is not final, failure is not fatal: it is the courage to continue that counts." - Winston Churchill

James Dyson

Sir James Dyson's story of success is a great example of how persistence and resilience in the face of failure can lead to great achievements. Dyson's journey began in the 1970s when he noticed that his conventional vacuum cleaner was losing suction power as the bag filled with dust. This led him to begin experimenting with different designs and technologies to create a better vacuum cleaner.

Over the next few years, Dyson built and tested over 5,000 prototypes of his vacuum cleaner, each one slightly different from the last. He faced numerous challenges, including the cost of materials, the complexity of the design, and the lack of interest from manufacturers. However, he persevered and continued to refine his designs until he finally came up with a working prototype.

Despite the initial success of his vacuum cleaner, Dyson struggled to find a manufacturer who was willing to produce it. He approached several companies but was turned down each time. However, he refused to give up on his dream and eventually founded his own company, Dyson Ltd, in 1993.

The launch of Dyson's bagless vacuum cleaner was a huge commercial success, and the company went on to develop a wide range of innovative household appliances, including air purifiers, hair dryers, and hand dryers. Dyson's net worth is now estimated to be over $20 billion, and his company is considered to be one of the most successful home appliance brands in the world.

Dyson's experience serves as an example of the value of tenacity and fortitude in the face of setbacks. He encountered several obstacles and rejections, yet he never lost faith in his idea and kept striving to achieve his objective. His success is a reminder that failure is not fatal, and that the courage to continue in the face of adversity is what ultimately counts.

"If you want to live a happy life, tie it to a goal, not to people or things." - Albert Einstein

Steve Jobs

When Steve Jobs was a college dropout, he decided to take a class in calligraphy. It was not something he needed to do or that he thought would lead to anything, but he was interested in the art of typography. He learned about different typefaces and how they were created, and he was fascinated by the beauty and intricacy of the letters.

Years later, when Jobs was developing the first Macintosh computer, he drew on his knowledge of calligraphy to create a new and innovative font system. The Macintosh was the first computer to offer multiple typefaces, and it was a huge success. This feature set it apart from other computers and helped to establish Apple's brand identity.

Looking back on this experience, Jobs said, "If I had never dropped in on that single course in college, the Mac would have never had multiple typefaces or proportionally spaced fonts." He went on to explain that it was impossible to connect the dots looking forward, but that everything made sense looking backwards. He had followed his passion for calligraphy, not knowing where it would lead, and it had ultimately helped him to create something that would change the world.

This story serves as an excellent example of how happiness should be linked to a goal rather than to other people or things. Jobs didn't know what he wanted to do with his life when he dropped out of college, but he trusted his passion for calligraphy and pursued it. By doing so, he was able to make a profound impact on the world of technology and create a legacy that will be remembered for years to come.

"You can't build a reputation on what you are going to do." - Henry Ford

Charles G. Conn

Charles G. Conn was a man who had a passion for music and was a talented performer on various brass instruments, including the cornet, which was a popular instrument in the late 1800s. In 1876, he founded the C.G. Conn Company in Elkhart, Indiana, with the aim of making high-quality brass instruments.

However, Conn had no experience as a manufacturer, and he was not particularly skilled in the art of instrument making. Nevertheless, he was convinced that he could create the best band instruments in the world and set about making bold promises to his potential customers.

He declared that his instruments would be "as perfect as human skill can make them" and that he would spare no expense to achieve this goal. He promised that his instruments would be made with the finest materials, that every part would be precision-crafted, and that they would be free of defects.

Conn was able to persuade some clients to order his instruments despite his lack of experience by relying only on his promises. He collected deposits from these orders and used the money to buy the necessary equipment and raw materials to start production.

But when Conn started shipping out his instruments, his clients frequently expressed disappointment. The instruments were of poor quality and did not live up to his promises. Many customers canceled their orders or returned their instruments for a refund.

Conn tried to improve the quality of his instruments, but he was never able to deliver on his promises to create the best band instruments in the world. His reputation suffered as a result, and his business struggled for years to come.

This anecdote illustrates the quote "You can't build a reputation on what you are going to do" because Conn's promises and bold claims were not enough to establish his reputation as a manufacturer of high-quality instruments. He had to deliver on his promises and consistently provide high-quality products to earn the trust and respect of his customers.

"I have not failed. I've just found 10,000 ways that won't work." - Thomas Edison

Grace Hopper

Grace Hopper was born in New York City in 1906 and earned a degree in mathematics from Vassar College in 1928. She went on to earn a master's degree and a PhD in mathematics from Yale University, becoming one of the first women to earn a PhD in mathematics from the institution.

In 1943, during World War II, Hopper decided to join the war effort and was assigned to work on the Mark I computer at Harvard University. The Mark I was a massive, electromechanical computer that was used by the U.S. Navy for calculations related to ballistics.

On September 9, 1945, the Mark I experienced a malfunction that Hopper and her team spent hours trying to identify. Eventually, they discovered that a moth had gotten caught in one of the relays, causing the machine to malfunction. Hopper removed the moth and taped it into the logbook with the annotation, "First actual case of bug being found." The term "debugging" has been used ever since to refer to the process of finding and fixing errors in computer programs.

After the war, Hopper continued to work on computers, developing the first compiler, which translated programming languages into machine code. She was also instrumental in the development of the COBOL programming language, which is still in use today.

Throughout her career, Hopper demonstrated a tenacity and persistence similar to that of Thomas Edison. She was known for saying, "The most dangerous phrase in the language is, 'We've always done it this way.'" Instead of accepting the status quo, Hopper was always looking for new and better ways to do things.

"The only way to do great work is to love what you do." - Steve Jobs

Ed Catmull

In the early 1980s, Pixar was a small computer graphics company that had been spun off from Lucasfilm. They had some success creating animations for television commercials, but they wanted to create a short film that would demonstrate the potential of computer animation for storytelling.

The team, led by Ed Catmull and John Lasseter, decided to create a short film called "Luxo Jr." that would tell the story of a pair of desk lamps. It was a simple concept, but the challenge was in creating convincing, expressive characters using computer animation, which was still a relatively new field at the time.

The group spent months on the project, but they had trouble getting the lamps to light up. The animation was stiff and robotic, and the team was getting frustrated. Catmull realized that they needed a new approach, so he called a meeting with the team and told them to take a break from the project.

During the break, Catmull encouraged the team to experiment and play with new ideas. Some of the animators started creating their own short films, while others pursued new hobbies and interests. Catmull himself spent some time tinkering with a new computer program that he had been working on.

When they returned to "Luxo Jr." a few weeks later, the animators were refreshed and reinvigorated. They had a newfound sense of joy and excitement about the project, and they approached the animation with renewed energy and passion. They began to experiment with new techniques and ideas, and eventually came up with a breakthrough in computer animation that allowed them to create more expressive and convincing characters.

The result was a short film that not only demonstrated the potential of computer animation for storytelling, but also earned an Academy Award nomination and helped put Pixar on the map as a leading animation studio.

What this anecdote shows is that sometimes the best way to overcome creative challenges is not to push harder or work longer hours, but to take a step back and approach the problem from a new perspective. When you love what you do, you can find new inspiration and energy by experimenting, playing, and pursuing your interests, and that can lead to breakthroughs and great work.

"Be the change you wish to see in the world." - Mahatma Gandhi

Richard Feynman

Richard Feynman was a renowned physicist who was a member of the Presidential Commission on the Space Shuttle Challenger Accident in the early 1980s. After the Challenger exploded in 1986, the commission was tasked with investigating the causes of the disaster. Feynman was known for his ability to explain complex scientific concepts in a simple and accessible way, and he quickly became an important member of the commission.

As Feynman began to investigate the causes of the disaster, he became increasingly concerned about the reliability of the O-ring seals that were used in the solid rocket boosters. These seals were designed to prevent hot gases from escaping from the booster and damaging the rest of the spacecraft. However, Feynman discovered that the O-rings were vulnerable to low temperatures, which could cause them to fail and lead to a catastrophic explosion.

To demonstrate the vulnerability of the O-rings, Feynman conducted a simple experiment during a televised hearing of the commission. He placed a small piece of the O-ring material in a glass of ice water and then showed that the rubber became hard and inflexible in the cold. He then demonstrated that the same material became flexible and resilient when warmed up.

Feynman's demonstration had a powerful impact on the commission and the public. It showed that the O-ring material was not suitable for use in the low temperatures of that morning and that this was a key factor in the disaster. Feynman's willingness to engage in hands-on investigation and to share his findings with the public helped to change the way NASA operated and ultimately made the space program safer.

Feynman's commitment to understanding and improving the world around him is an embodiment of the idea that we should "be the change we wish to see in the world." Rather than simply accepting the status quo, Feynman took action to make a difference and ultimately helped to make the world a safer place.

"The only limit to our realization of tomorrow will be our doubts of today."
- Franklin D. Roosevelt

Douglas Engelbart

Douglas Engelbart was a computer scientist who worked in Silicon Valley during the 1960s. At a time when computers were still large and unwieldy machines that could only be operated by experts, Engelbart had a vision for a computer that could augment human intelligence and help people work together more effectively.

Engelbart believed that computers could be used to solve some of the world's most pressing problems, such as poverty, hunger, and war. He saw them as a tool for collaboration and collective intelligence, allowing people to work together to achieve great things.

However, many of Engelbart's colleagues and investors thought he was crazy. They didn't see the value in his ideas, and they doubted that computers could ever be as powerful as he envisioned. Engelbart struggled to find funding and support for his work, and he often had to work in secret to avoid being ridiculed by his peers.

Engelbart persisted in spite of the skepticism of others. He spent years developing new technologies that would allow people to interact with computers in new and intuitive ways. He invented the first computer mouse, which allowed users to point and click on objects on the screen, and he created new ways of organizing and sharing information using hypertext.

Engelbart's greatest achievement was the creation of the first online network, which he called the "Augmentation Research Center." The network allowed researchers to share information and collaborate on projects from remote locations, paving the way for the modern internet.

In 1968, Engelbart gave a now-famous demo of his work at a conference in San Francisco. The demo showcased many of the technologies that we take for granted today, including the mouse, videoconferencing, and hypertext. It was a vision of the future that few people had imagined, and it inspired a generation of computer scientists and entrepreneurs to create new technologies that continue to shape our world today.

Engelbart's story is a powerful reminder that doubt can be a powerful force, but it's not an insurmountable one. When we have a vision for the future and believe in ourselves, we can overcome even the greatest obstacles and achieve great things.

"Don't let yesterday take up too much of today." - Will Rogers

Walter Mischel

In the late 1960s, Walter Mischel, a psychologist at Stanford University, conducted a series of experiments on self-control with preschool children. In one of these experiments, he offered the children a choice between a small reward, such as one marshmallow, that they could have immediately, or a larger reward, such as two marshmallows, if they were willing to wait for a short period of time (usually about 15 minutes). Mischel found that some children were able to resist the temptation of the immediate reward and wait for the larger reward, while others could not.

One of the children who participated in Mischel's experiment was a four-year-old girl named Tanya. Tanya was a bright and cheerful child, but she struggled to resist the temptation of the marshmallow. She would look at the marshmallow, touch it, and smell it, but she could not resist eating it.

Mischel noticed that Tanya had a unique strategy for dealing with the temptation. Instead of focusing on the marshmallow she couldn't have, Tanya distracted herself by singing songs and playing games. She would talk to herself and pretend that the marshmallow was just a picture or a cloud. By taking her mind off the marshmallow, Tanya was able to wait for the larger reward.

Years later, when Tanya was a teenager, Mischel visited her at her home. He asked her if she remembered the marshmallow test, and Tanya replied that she did. Mischel asked her what strategies she used to resist the temptation, and Tanya explained that she had learned to focus on the present moment and not let her past experiences dictate her behavior. She said, "I just thought, 'Don't worry about what happened yesterday. Just worry about what you're doing right now.'"

Tanya's ability to focus on the present moment and not let past experiences dictate her behavior is a great example of how we can apply Will Rogers' quote in our own lives. By letting go of the past and focusing on what we can do in the present, we can make better decisions and achieve our goals.

"Success is walking from failure to failure with no loss of enthusiasm." - Winston Churchill

Thomas Edison

During the late 1800s, Thomas Edison and his team were engaged in the development of an electric light bulb that was both practical and efficient. However, the process was long and arduous, with the team encountering numerous obstacles and setbacks along the way.

Edison famously said, "I have not failed. I've just found 10,000 ways that won't work," referring to the many unsuccessful attempts at creating a working light bulb. Despite the setbacks, Edison remained enthusiastic and determined, working tirelessly to refine his ideas and develop new approaches.

In one particularly memorable incident, a journalist asked Edison how it felt to have failed 1,000 times in his attempts to create the light bulb. Edison replied, "I didn't fail 1,000 times. The light bulb was an invention with 1,000 steps."

This quote captures Edison's attitude towards failure - rather than seeing each setback as a failure, he viewed each attempt as a step closer to achieving success. Edison was persistent, refusing to give up in the face of adversity, and he ultimately succeeded in developing a practical and efficient electric light bulb that would change the world.

The example of Edison serves as a potent reminder that success is not the result of a string of flawless successes, but rather of tenacity and fortitude in the face of setbacks. By embracing his failures and refusing to give up, Edison was able to turn his vision into a reality, and his example serves as an inspiration to this day.

"Believe in yourself and all that you are. Know that there is something inside you that is greater than any obstacle." - Christian D. Larson

Michael Jordan

Michael Jordan's story of perseverance and self-belief began in his sophomore year of high school when he tried out for the varsity basketball team. Despite his talent and love for the sport, he was cut from the team by the coach, who felt he was too small and not ready for the varsity level.

Jordan was devastated but refused to give up on his dream. Instead, he worked even harder to improve his skills, practicing every day on his own and with his friends. He also joined the junior varsity team and put in a standout performance, scoring an average of 25 points per game.

By his junior year, Jordan had grown taller and stronger, and his skills had improved significantly. He tried out again for the varsity team and this time, he made the cut. He went on to lead his team to the state championship and earned a scholarship to play at the University of North Carolina.

Jordan continued to work hard and believe in himself throughout his college career, where he led his team to a national championship and earned a reputation as one of the best players in the country. He was drafted by the Chicago Bulls in 1984, and the rest, as they say, is history.

Throughout his professional career, Jordan faced many challenges and obstacles, including injuries, tough opponents, and personal setbacks. However, he never gave up, and his self-belief and determination helped him overcome these challenges and become one of the greatest basketball players of all time.

Jordan's narrative is a compelling illustration of how self-confidence, diligent effort, and unwavering determination can empower us to reach our aspirations and surmount any hurdle that we encounter. It reminds us that we all have the potential to do great things if we believe in ourselves and are willing to put in the effort to make our dreams a reality.

"Success is not how high you have climbed, but how you make a positive difference to the world." - Roy T. Bennett

Paul Farmer

Paul Farmer's work in Haiti began in the early 1980s when he was a young medical student. While working in the clinics there, he was shocked by the lack of basic healthcare resources and the devastating impact that poverty was having on the health of the local population.

Over the next several years, Farmer continued to visit Haiti and work in the clinics there. He eventually founded the nonprofit organization Partners in Health (PIH) in 1987, along with a group of colleagues, with the goal of providing medical care and resources to the poor in Haiti.

PIH's approach to healthcare is unique in that it focuses on long-term solutions and prioritizes the needs of patients. The organization works to build strong healthcare systems in communities, training local healthcare workers and building clinics and hospitals where they are needed most. PIH also works to address the root causes of illness, such as poverty, malnutrition, and lack of access to clean water and sanitation.

Through his work with PIH, Farmer has helped to make a significant impact on the health and well-being of people in Haiti and other countries around the world. The organization has been involved in a number of groundbreaking initiatives, such as successfully treating drug-resistant tuberculosis in Peru and developing a model for HIV care and treatment in Rwanda that has been replicated in other countries.

In addition to his work with PIH, Farmer has also written extensively on global health issues and has served as an advisor to numerous world leaders. He has been recognized with a number of prestigious awards and honors for his work, including a MacArthur Foundation "genius grant" and the Presidential Medal of Freedom.

Overall, Paul Farmer's dedication to improving the health and well-being of the world's most vulnerable populations is a powerful example of how success can be measured not just by personal achievements, but by the positive impact one can make on the world.

"It's not about how hard you hit. It's about how hard you can get hit and keep moving forward." - Rocky Balboa (fictional character played by Sylvester Stallone)

Amy Van Dyken

Amy Van Dyken, hailing from Englewood, Colorado, was born in 1973 and commenced her competitive swimming journey at a tender age. She was a talented swimmer from the start, and by the time she was in high school, she had already won several national titles. In college, she swam for the Arizona State University team and continued to rack up victories.

Van Dyken's biggest success came at the 1996 Atlanta Olympics, where she won four gold medals - in the 50-meter freestyle, the 100-meter butterfly, the 4x100-meter freestyle relay, and the 4x100-meter medley relay. She was hailed as a national hero, and her career seemed to be on an upward trajectory.

However, just two months after the Olympics, Van Dyken was involved in a serious ATV accident. She was driving with a friend when she hit a curb and was thrown from the vehicle. The accident severed her spinal cord at the T11 vertebra, leaving her paralyzed from the waist down.

The injury was devastating for Van Dyken, who was used to relying on her physical abilities to succeed. She was hospitalized for several weeks and underwent surgery to stabilize her spine. When she was released from the hospital, she faced a long road to recovery and a new reality of living with a disability.

In spite of the obstacles, Van Dyken was resolute in her decision not to allow her injury to shape her identity. She began a grueling rehabilitation program, working to regain her strength and independence. She also worked with doctors and physical therapists to develop a new training regimen that would allow her to continue swimming at a high level.

Her new training program focused on upper body strength and cardiovascular fitness, since she could no longer use her legs to kick. She also had to adapt her technique to compensate for her limited mobility. She began training in a specially-designed pool with a hydraulic lift that would lower her into the water and raise her back out.

Within a year of the accident, Van Dyken was back in the pool, swimming with the help of a floatation device. She continued to work hard, and within two years, she was back competing at the highest level. At the 2000 Sydney Olympics, she won two more gold medals - in the 4x100-meter freestyle relay and the 4x100-meter medley relay - and became the most successful American athlete at the Games.

Van Dyken retired from swimming in 2002, but her resilience and determination continue to inspire people around the world. She has become an advocate for people with spinal cord injuries and has worked to raise awareness of the challenges they face. Her story shows that it's not about how hard you hit, but about how hard you can get hit and keep moving forward.

"The difference between ordinary and extraordinary is that little extra." - Jimmy Johnson

Derek Redmond

Derek Redmond was a British athlete who had set the world record in the 4x400 meters relay, and he was considered a strong contender for a medal in the 400-meter race at the 1992 Olympics. During the semi-finals, just 250 meters into the race, Redmond suddenly pulled up with a torn hamstring and fell to the ground in agony.

Redmond endured intense pain but still refused to be carried off on a stretcher. He was determined to finish the race no matter what. He stood up and began to hobble along the track, his left leg completely useless. The crowd watched in stunned silence as Redmond gritted his teeth and continued to move forward, one agonizing step at a time.

Then, something truly extraordinary happened. Redmond's father, Jim, who had been watching the race from the stands, suddenly broke through security and ran onto the track to be with his son. Together, they continued to move towards the finish line, with Jim's arm around his son's waist, supporting him.

As they approached the finish line, the crowd rose to their feet and began to applaud and cheer. Redmond and his father finally crossed the line, with Derek falling into his father's arms, sobbing. It was a moment of pure emotion and triumph, and it showed that the difference between ordinary and extraordinary is that little extra effort, the determination to push past your limits, and the courage to keep going no matter what.

"The best way to predict the future is to create it." - Peter Drucker

Steve Wozniak

Steve Jobs and Steve Wozniak, the co-founders of Apple, are widely regarded as pioneers in the personal computer industry. In the early days of computing, mainframe computers were the norm, and few people could have predicted the rise of the personal computer. However, Jobs and Wozniak saw the potential for a new kind of computing, and they set out to make it a reality.

Wozniak had been working on a new computer design in his spare time while employed at Hewlett-Packard (HP). He showed his prototype to Jobs, who immediately recognized its potential as a product. Jobs convinced Wozniak to leave HP and start a new company with him, and together they founded Apple Computer in 1976.

Their first product was the Apple I, which was little more than a circuit board that could be connected to a keyboard and monitor. While it was not a commercial success, it set the stage for their next product, the Apple II.

The Apple II was a more polished product that was designed to be more user-friendly and accessible to the general public. It was one of the first personal computers to come with a color display and a built-in keyboard, and it was relatively affordable compared to the mainframe computers of the time. This made it a popular choice for home users and small businesses.

The success of the Apple II allowed Apple to become a major player in the personal computer industry. It also paved the way for other companies to enter the market and create their own personal computers. This, in turn, led to the personal computing revolution of the 1980s, which saw personal computers become more powerful, affordable, and accessible to the general public.

The story of Apple and the personal computer industry is a great example of how the best way to predict the future is to create it. Jobs and Wozniak could have simply observed the trends in the computing industry and made educated guesses about where it was heading. Instead, they actively participated in shaping the future of computing by creating a product that was both innovative and accessible. By doing so, they were able to predict the future of computing and shape it themselves.

"You can have everything in life you want, if you will just help other people get what they want." - Zig Ziglar

Kat Cole

Kat Cole grew up in Jacksonville, Florida, and dropped out of high school at the age of 17. She worked a variety of jobs, including as a Hooters waitress, before being offered an opportunity to work for a new company, Cinnabon.

The man who offered her the job, Rich, was a regular at the Hooters where she worked, and he saw something in her that he believed would make her a great addition to his new company. He offered her a position as a hostess, with the promise of opportunities for advancement.

Kat quickly embraced the opportunity and threw herself into learning everything she could about the business. She would arrive early, stay late, and take on extra responsibilities, such as cleaning the kitchen and taking out the trash, to show her commitment to the job.

Through her hard work, dedication, and willingness to help others, Kat was able to quickly climb the ranks at Cinnabon. She was promoted to a management position within a year, and continued to excel in her role. She learned about baking, marketing, and management, and became a key player in the company's growth and success.

Kat was known for her willingness to help her colleagues and employees, even when it wasn't part of her job description. She would often work long hours to help with training, or to help open a new store. Her dedication and work ethic earned her the respect and admiration of her coworkers and superiors.

Kat continued to rise through the ranks at Cinnabon, eventually becoming vice president of the company. In this role, she oversaw the company's international expansion and was instrumental in its success. She continued to focus on helping others, empowering her team and colleagues to achieve their own goals and dreams.

In 2010, Kat left Cinnabon to become the president of Cinnabon's parent company, FOCUS Brands. In this role, she oversaw the company's growth and expansion, which included the acquisition of several other well-known brands.

Today, Kat is the CEO of FOCUS Brands, and is widely respected as a business leader and a role model for young people. Her story is often cited as an example of how hard work, dedication, and a willingness to help others can lead to incredible success.

Kat Cole's narrative highlights that through hard work, wholehearted commitment to one's job, and assisting others in reaching their own ambitions, one can attain remarkable triumph in their professional life. Her success story is a testament to the power of a strong work ethic, a desire to learn and grow, and a willingness to help others along the way.

"Do not wait to strike till the iron is hot; but make it hot by striking." - William B. Sprague

Travis Kalanick and Garrett Camp

In 2008, Travis Kalanick and Garrett Camp were attending a tech conference in Paris when they had the idea for a smartphone app that would allow people to easily hail a taxi using their mobile device. They realized that this could solve a major pain point for people trying to hail a cab, and they started brainstorming how they could turn their idea into a business.

After returning to San Francisco, Kalanick and Camp founded a company called UberCab (later renamed to simply "Uber") and started working on their app. However, they hesitated to launch the app, waiting for the "perfect time" to enter the market.

As they were waiting, they realized that they were not the only ones who had thought of this idea. Competitors were starting to emerge, such as Lyft and Sidecar. Kalanick and Camp also faced regulatory hurdles, as taxi companies and government officials were not yet sure how to deal with ride-sharing services.

Despite these challenges, Kalanick and Camp decided to take action and launch their app in San Francisco in 2010. They did not have permission from taxi regulators, but they believed that their service could solve a major problem for consumers and that they could work out the regulatory issues later.

The initial launch was a success, and Uber quickly gained a following. Customers appreciated the convenience and reliability of the service, and drivers appreciated the flexibility and earning potential. As Uber continued to expand to new cities, it faced opposition from taxi companies and government regulators, but the company was able to overcome these obstacles and continue growing.

By taking action and "striking" while the idea was still hot, Kalanick and Camp were able to build a successful business that revolutionized the transportation industry. Today, Uber is a household name and has expanded to offer a variety of services beyond ride-sharing, such as food delivery and electric bikes and scooters.

"Don't let what you cannot do interfere with what you can do." - John Wooden

Rick Hoyt

Rick Hoyt was diagnosed with cerebral palsy at birth, which left him unable to speak or walk. Doctors told his parents that he would never be able to communicate or live a normal life. Despite this, Rick's parents were determined to help him live as full a life as possible.

When Rick was young, his parents worked with a team of specialists to develop a communication system that would allow him to communicate using his eyes. They also encouraged him to participate in sports and other activities, even though he was limited by his physical abilities.

When Rick was a teenager, he asked his father, Dick, if they could participate in a charity race to benefit a local student who had been paralyzed in an accident. Dick agreed, and they completed the 5-mile race together. It was a difficult challenge, but they finished, and Rick loved the experience.

Over the years, Dick and Rick went on to complete hundreds of races and marathons together, using a specially-designed wheelchair that allowed Dick to push Rick through the course. They even completed a full Ironman triathlon together, with Dick swimming, biking, and running while pulling Rick behind him in a raft and on a special bike.

Through it all, Rick never let his physical limitations interfere with his ability to enjoy life and achieve great things. His story is a powerful reminder that we should focus on what we can do, even when faced with seemingly insurmountable obstacles.

"If you can't fly then run, if you can't run then walk, if you can't walk then crawl, but whatever you do you have to keep moving forward." - Martin Luther King Jr.

Ann Bancroft

In 1984, Ann Bancroft and Liv Arnesen set out on a historic expedition to become the first women to reach the North Pole on foot. They planned to travel across the Arctic ice from northern Canada to the Pole, a distance of over 1,000 miles.

The journey was extremely difficult, with temperatures sometimes dropping below -40 degrees Fahrenheit and strong winds creating dangerous conditions. The women faced many challenges along the way, including equipment failures, injuries, and fatigue.

One of the most difficult moments came when the team was trapped in their tent for five days due to a blizzard. They were forced to wait out the storm, which battered their tent with high winds and snow, leaving them with limited supplies and no way to travel.

When the blizzard finally subsided, Bancroft and Arnesen emerged to find that their equipment was frozen and their food supplies were running low. They had to improvise in order to survive, melting snow for drinking water and carefully rationing their remaining food.

Despite these setbacks, the team never lost sight of their goal. They continued to travel north, using skis to glide over the ice when conditions allowed, and crawling forward on hands and knees when necessary.

After 56 days of grueling travel, Bancroft and Arnesen finally reached the North Pole on May 13, 1986. They had become the first women to complete the journey on foot and had overcome incredible obstacles to achieve their goal.

Ann Bancroft later reflected on the journey, saying, "We just kept moving forward. We did what we had to do to survive and make it to the Pole. It wasn't always pretty, but we never gave up." Her story is a powerful reminder of the importance of perseverance and determination in the face of adversity.

"Chase the vision, not the money, the money will end up following you." - Tony Hsieh

Elon Musk

In the early 2000s, Elon Musk was working on his latest venture, SpaceX, with the goal of reducing the cost of space exploration and ultimately making humanity a multi-planetary species. He was convinced that humanity needed to become a "multi-planetary species" in order to safeguard its future and to ensure that life could continue to thrive even in the event of a global catastrophe.

At the time, Musk had already made a fortune through the sale of his previous startup, PayPal, but he was pouring all of his time, energy, and money into SpaceX. He invested nearly all of his personal wealth, an estimated $100 million, into the company, and even went so far as to take out loans against his own assets to keep the company afloat.

Musk encountered multiple setbacks, such as several rocket failures and a near-bankruptcy, yet he remained devoted to his vision of democratizing space exploration and making it more affordable and accessible. He was convinced that by developing reusable rockets and reducing the cost of launches, space exploration could become more economically viable.

In 2008, NASA awarded SpaceX a $1.6 billion contract to transport cargo and eventually astronauts to the International Space Station. This was a major milestone for the company, and it helped establish SpaceX as a major player in the aerospace industry. However, the company continued to face challenges, including a rocket explosion in 2015 that destroyed a cargo ship intended for the ISS.

These setbacks notwithstanding, Musk remained steadfast in his commitment to his vision of transforming humanity into a multi-planetary civilization. He continued to invest in the company, and his efforts ultimately paid off. In 2020, SpaceX successfully launched its first crewed mission to the ISS, marking a major milestone in human space exploration.

Today, SpaceX is one of the most successful and innovative aerospace companies in the world. Its reusable rockets and low-cost launch capabilities have revolutionized the industry, and the company is now working on developing the technologies necessary to enable human colonization of Mars.

The main lesson to take away from this is that Musk was able to create a prosperous company that has revolutionized the aerospace industry and is making human space travel a realistic possibility for the future by pursuing his vision and investing all of his resources into it.

"You don't have to be great to start, but you have to start to be great." - Zig Ziglar

Jimi Hendrix

Born in Seattle, Washington, in 1942, Jimi Hendrix exhibited an innate musical ability from his early years and began playing the guitar at a tender age. However, as a young adult, Hendrix struggled to make a name for himself in the music industry. He played in various bands, but never found much success, and eventually he joined the army.

After serving in the army for a year, Hendrix was discharged due to a medical condition. He returned to Seattle and continued to play music, but he struggled to gain traction. In 1961, he moved to New York City, where he played in various clubs and bars, but he still couldn't break through.

In 1966, Hendrix was discovered by Chas Chandler, the bassist for the British band The Animals. Chandler was struck by Hendrix's unique guitar playing and offered to take him to London to help him get his career off the ground.

Hendrix accepted Chandler's offer and moved to London in September 1966. There, Chandler introduced him to a number of record labels and producers, but they were initially skeptical of Hendrix's music. They didn't think it would be successful, and they didn't know how to market it.

Undeterred, Chandler set up a recording session for Hendrix to showcase his talents. At the session, Hendrix played a number of his original songs, including "Hey Joe," "Stone Free," and

"Purple Haze." His playing was unlike anything the producers had heard before, and they were impressed.

Soon after the recording session, Hendrix was signed to a record deal with Track Records. In May 1967, he released his first single, "Hey Joe," which was a hit in the UK. He followed it up with "Purple Haze," which became a massive hit, launching his career.

Over the next few years, Hendrix released a number of groundbreaking albums, including "Are You Experienced," "Axis: Bold as Love," and "Electric Ladyland." He became known for his incredible guitar skills, his innovative use of feedback and distortion, and his unique style.

Although his career was brief, Hendrix is widely recognized as one of the most exceptional guitarists in history. His music continues to inspire new generations of musicians, and his legacy endures to this day.

Hendrix's story teaches us that he wasn't an instant sensation, but he was willing to take a leap of faith and pursue his dream. By taking that initial step, he was able to attain unparalleled success and leave a lasting impact in the realm of music.

"The only person you are destined to become is the person you decide to be."
- Ralph Waldo Emerson

J.K. Rowling

Joanne Rowling, who later became known as J.K. Rowling, was a struggling single mother living on welfare in Edinburgh, Scotland when she began writing the first Harry Potter book, "Harry Potter and the Philosopher's Stone." She would often write in local cafes while her baby daughter slept in a stroller next to her.

Despite her difficult circumstances, Rowling was determined to become a successful writer. She spent years working on the manuscript for "Harry Potter," and after completing it, she sent the manuscript to several publishers. But the book was rejected multiple times before Bloomsbury agreed to publish it in 1997.

Even after securing a publishing deal, Rowling's challenges were far from over. She faced the death of her mother, who had always encouraged her writing, and struggled with depression. However, she continued to work hard and make decisions that would help her achieve her goals.

Rowling's determination and perseverance paid off, and "Harry Potter and the Philosopher's Stone" became an international sensation, launching a multi-billion-dollar franchise that included seven books, eight movies, and numerous other spin-off products. Today, Rowling is one of the best-selling authors of all time, and her success serves as a powerful reminder that we have the power to shape our own destinies through the decisions we make and the actions we take.

"I've missed more than 9,000 shots in my career. I've lost almost 300 games. 26 times, I've been trusted to take the game winning shot and missed. I've failed over and over and over again in my life. And that is why I succeed." - Michael Jordan

Kobe Bryant

In the 1997 NBA playoffs, Kobe Bryant was a young player in only his second season with the Los Angeles Lakers. Despite his relative inexperience, Bryant was known for his confidence and his willingness to take big shots. In Game 5 of the Western Conference semifinals against the Utah Jazz, the Lakers found themselves in a tight contest with the Jazz, and Bryant had a chance to be the hero.

With just a few seconds left on the clock and the Lakers down by three points, Bryant received the ball on the right wing, faked a shot to get his defender in the air, and then attempted a three-pointer to tie the game. The shot missed, and the Jazz held on to win the game and eliminate the Lakers from the playoffs.

After the game, Bryant was visibly upset and took the loss hard. He later said that he didn't sleep for two days after the game and that he watched the tape of his missed shot over and over again. However, he also said that he used the moment as motivation to work harder and become a better player.

Over the next several seasons, Bryant did just that. He continued to work on his game, improving his shooting, his defense, and his all-around skills. He also became more of a team player, learning to trust his teammates and become a better leader. In 2000, Bryant won his first NBA championship with the Lakers, and he would go on to win four more over the course of his career. He also won numerous individual awards, including the NBA MVP award in 2008.

In many ways, Kobe Bryant's experience is a perfect example of Michael Jordan's quote. Bryant missed the game-winning shot, but he didn't let that failure define him or his career. Instead, he used it as motivation to work harder and become a better player. He failed over and over again, but he kept coming back and ultimately succeeded, becoming one of the greatest players in NBA history.

"The only way to get started is to quit talking and begin doing." - Walt Disney

Kevin Systrom

Kevin Systrom, the co-founder of Instagram, had an idea for a photo-sharing app called Burbn while he was working as a product manager at Google. He started working on the app in his spare time and eventually showed it to his friend, Mike Krieger. Krieger was impressed by the app and suggested that they work on it together.

Systrom and Krieger spent several months refining their idea, discussing features, and planning the development of the app. However, they didn't actually start building the app until they attended the startup incubator Baseline in San Francisco.

At Baseline, Systrom and Krieger were surrounded by other entrepreneurs who were all actively working on their own projects. The sense of urgency and the fast-paced environment inspired Systrom and Krieger to stop talking about their idea and start building it.

They realized that they needed to focus on the core features of the app and create a simple, easy-to-use interface. They also decided to change the name of the app from Burbn to Instagram.

With a renewed sense of purpose and determination, Systrom and Krieger worked around the clock to develop the app. They launched Instagram in October 2010, and within hours, they had thousands of users.

Instagram quickly became a massive success, and by April 2012, Facebook acquired the app for $1 billion. Systrom and Krieger's ability to take action and turn their idea into a reality was a key factor in the app's success.

The story highlights that having a good idea is just the beginning, as taking action and putting in the work is crucial for success. Sometimes it takes a shift in surroundings or a feeling of pressure to prompt you to take that first step, but once you do, you're on your way to realizing your vision. The key is to start building and keep going until your idea becomes a reality.

"There is no substitute for hard work." - Thomas Edison

Walt Disney

In 1901, Walt Disney was born in Chicago, Illinois, and displayed a proclivity for drawing from an early age, spending much of his youth crafting sketches and cartoons. After serving in the Red Cross during World War I, Disney returned to the United States and began working as a commercial artist.

In the early 1920s, Disney moved to California and began pursuing a career in animation. He landed a job at the Kansas City Film Ad Company, where he met a fellow artist named Ub Iwerks. Together, the two men began experimenting with new animation techniques, and they eventually developed a new style that involved creating more realistic characters and using synchronized sound.

In 1928, Disney had an idea for a new character, a plucky little mouse named Mickey. He drew sketches of the character and developed a story that involved Mickey saving his girlfriend Minnie from a runaway train. Disney worked tirelessly to bring the character to life, spending long hours in the studio and often sleeping on a cot in his office.

When the first Mickey Mouse cartoon, "Steamboat Willie," premiered in New York in November 1928, it was an instant sensation. The synchronized sound and the lovable character captured audiences' hearts, and Mickey quickly became a cultural icon. Over the next few years, Disney created a whole world around Mickey, developing other characters like Donald Duck and Goofy and producing dozens of cartoons.

But in 1929, just as Mickey was becoming a huge success, Disney received a devastating blow. The distributor he had been working with, Charles Mintz, secretly hired away all of his animators and stole the rights to Oswald the Lucky Rabbit, a character that Disney had created for Mintz's studio. Disney was left with nothing.

At first, Disney was devastated. But he quickly realized that he had the skills and the vision to create something even better. He called a meeting with his remaining staff and told them that they were going to create a new character, one that would be even more memorable and beloved than Oswald. He instructed them to work harder than ever before and to pour all of their creativity and passion into the new project.

For the next few months, Disney and his team worked tirelessly on the new character. They experimented with new techniques and developed a story that would showcase the character's strengths. They stayed up all night, often working in shifts, and poured all of their energy and talent into the project.

The hard work paid off. In 1930, the first Mickey Mouse comic strip was published, and it was an instant hit. Over the next few years, Disney continued to develop the character and his world, producing cartoons, comic strips, and merchandise. Mickey Mouse became a cultural icon, and Disney became one of the most successful and influential animators of all time.

Through this story, we can see that there is no substitute for hard work. Disney's dedication to his craft and his willingness to put in the extra effort made all the difference in his success. Even when faced with setbacks and obstacles, he never gave up. Instead, he doubled down on his efforts and poured all of his energy into creating something even better.

"You are never too old to set another goal or to dream a new dream." - C.S. Lewis

Harland Sanders

Harland Sanders, who was born in Indiana, USA in 1890, experienced a challenging childhood and had to abandon his schooling in the 7th grade to provide for his family. Sanders held various jobs throughout his life, including as a farmhand, streetcar conductor, and soldier.

It wasn't until Sanders was in his 40s that he discovered his passion for cooking. He owned a gas station in Kentucky and began cooking meals for his customers using a pressure cooker to fry chicken. Sanders' chicken became incredibly popular, and soon people were coming from all over the area to taste it.

In 1952, Sanders decided to franchise his recipe and open a chain of fast-food restaurants called "Kentucky Fried Chicken." However, he faced numerous rejections from restaurant owners who were skeptical of his idea. In fact, he was turned down over 1,000 times before he finally found a partner who believed in his vision.

Even though he was in his 60s at the time, Sanders persisted in travelling across the country to promote his brand and refine his recipe. He even slept in his car on occasion to save money and keep the business afloat.

Eventually, Sanders' persistence paid off, and KFC began to gain popularity across the United States. In 1964, he sold the company for $2 million, but remained involved in the business as a spokesperson and ambassador for many years.

The story of Sanders proves that age should never be a barrier to pursuing your aspirations. Despite encountering several difficulties and obstacles, he persevered with his vision for KFC. Today, the fast-food chain he established is among the most prosperous and well-known in the world, with thousands of outlets across numerous countries.

"You miss 100% of the shots you don't take." - Michael Scott (fictional character played by Steve Carell)

David Vobora

David Vobora's story is a great example of taking a chance and making the most of an opportunity. In 2007, Vobora was a linebacker in the NFL, playing for the Seattle Seahawks. One day, he was approached by Staff Sgt. Travis Mills, a wounded Iraq War veteran who had lost all four of his limbs in an explosion.

Mills, who was recovering at a nearby military hospital, asked Vobora if he could help him work out. Vobora agreed, but he had no experience working with amputees and wasn't sure how to help Mills. However, he was determined to find a way to help Mills achieve his fitness goals.

Vobora spent months researching and experimenting with different workouts and equipment until he found a routine that worked for Mills. He used exercise bands, kettlebells, and other equipment to create a customized workout program that helped Mills build strength and improve his overall health.

Over time, Vobora's work with Mills led him to start a nonprofit called The Adaptive Training Foundation. The organization provides free personal training to people with physical disabilities, helping them to achieve their fitness goals and improve their quality of life.

Vobora's decision to take a chance and help Mills was a turning point in his life. If he had been too afraid to take on the challenge, he never would have discovered his passion for adaptive fitness and helped so many other people in the process.

The tale presented here vividly exemplifies the saying, "You miss 100% of the shots you don't take." Vobora, by seizing an opportunity, found himself embarking on a completely fresh career path with a newfound sense of direction. He could have easily turned Mills away, but instead he chose to take a risk and help someone in need. In doing so, he discovered a new calling and made a positive impact on the world.

"Believe in yourself, take on your challenges, dig deep within yourself to conquer fears. Never let anyone bring you down. You got this." - Chantal Sutherland

Wilma Rudolph

Wilma Rudolph was born prematurely in 1940 in Tennessee, USA. At the age of four, she contracted polio, which left her with a brace on her left leg and foot. Doctors told her mother that she would never walk again, but her mother refused to accept this and worked tirelessly with Wilma to help her overcome her physical challenges.

Wilma's family was poor, and she grew up in a segregated community where opportunities for African American children were limited. Despite this, she was determined to succeed, and she discovered a love for running in elementary school. She joined the school's track team and quickly became a standout athlete, setting records in the 50- and 100-yard dash.

In high school, Wilma continued to excel in track and field, but she faced discrimination and segregation when competing against white athletes. However, she remained focused on her goals and continued to train hard, even when she had to practice on gravel roads because her school did not have a track.

In 1956, at the age of 16, Wilma competed in the Olympic Games in Melbourne, Australia, but she did not win a medal. However, this experience fueled her determination to continue working hard and striving for greatness.

In 1960, Wilma qualified for the Olympic Games in Rome. Despite suffering from dehydration and exhaustion, she won the gold medal in the 100-meter dash, setting a world record in the process. She went on to win two more gold medals in the 200-meter dash and the 4x100-meter relay, becoming the first American woman to win three gold medals in a single Olympic Games.

Wilma's success inspired a generation of young athletes, and she went on to become a champion for civil rights and women's sports. She believed in the power of self-belief, hard work, and determination, and her story continues to inspire people around the world to this day.

"When you have a dream, you've got to grab it and never let go." - Carol Burnett

Elvis Presley

Elvis Presley's story of following his dream is a long and complex one, but it is a testament to the idea that success is not just a matter of talent or luck, but also of hard work, persistence, and dedication.

As a young boy, Elvis was deeply inspired by the music he heard on the radio and in church, and he soon became determined to become a musician himself. Despite facing numerous obstacles, such as a lack of resources, a difficult family life, and ridicule from his peers, Elvis remained focused on his goal and continued to hone his craft.

In 1953, when Elvis was just 18 years old, he saved up enough money to record his first demo at Sun Records in Memphis, Tennessee. Although the recording session was initially unsuccessful, Elvis continued to work on his music and eventually caught the attention of producer Sam Phillips, who recognized the young singer's potential and signed him to a recording contract.

Over the next few years, Elvis worked tirelessly to establish himself as a rising star in the music industry, performing at countless concerts and making numerous television appearances. He also faced criticism from some who dismissed his unique style of music as vulgar or inappropriate, but he refused to let these comments deter him from pursuing his dreams.

Throughout his career, Elvis continued to push himself to new heights, experimenting with different musical genres and refining his stage presence to captivate audiences. He also faced personal struggles, including a tumultuous love life, battles with addiction, and the pressures of fame, but he remained committed to his passion for music until his untimely death in 1977.

Elvis Presley's tale stands as a motivational illustration of what can be accomplished through a combination of hard work, dedication, and unwavering determination to pursue one's aspirations. Like Carol Burnett, he believed that with perseverance and determination, anyone can overcome obstacles and achieve their goals, no matter how challenging the path may be.

"Nothing is impossible. The word itself says 'I'm possible!'" - Audrey Hepburn

Roger Bannister

In the early 1950s, running a mile in less than four minutes was considered an impossible feat. Many people believed that it was physically impossible for the human body to run that fast, and most top athletes had given up trying to break the record.

But Roger Bannister, a British medical student and middle-distance runner, was determined to prove them wrong. He had been working on his running technique and training methods, and believed that he could become the first person to run a mile in under four minutes.

On May 6th, 1954, Bannister took to the track at Iffley Road in Oxford, England. The weather was poor, with strong winds and rain, but Bannister was determined to make history.

He set off at a fast pace, with two pacemakers running ahead of him to help him maintain his speed. Bannister reached the halfway mark in just under two minutes, but then started to feel the effects of the strong headwind.

With 300 meters to go, Bannister found the strength to push himself to the limit. He crossed the finish line in 3 minutes and 59.4 seconds, breaking the four-minute barrier for the first time in history.

Bannister's achievement was a turning point in the history of sport. It proved that the human body was capable of more than people had previously believed, and inspired other athletes to push themselves to new limits. Within a year, several other runners had also broken the four-minute barrier.

Bannister's accomplishment also showed that nothing is impossible if you believe in yourself and are willing to work hard to achieve your goals. The word "impossible" itself is just a combination of letters, and when you break it down, you realize that it's really just "I'm possible!"

"There is nothing impossible to they who will try." - Alexander the Great

James Farny

James Farny's obsession with finding a solution to Dow Chemical's problem began in the late 1950s when the company was developing a new type of rubber that they called "silicone rubber." This rubber was unlike any other rubber known at the time, as it could withstand extreme temperatures and was resistant to water, oxygen, and many chemicals. However, the company was facing a major problem in their production process. They needed to make the silicone rubber in large sheets, but every time they tried, the sheets would tear apart.

Farny was a young scientist working in Dow Chemical's newly established silicone rubber lab, and he was tasked with finding a solution to the tearing problem. He spent countless hours in the lab, experimenting with different methods and materials, but nothing seemed to work. He became increasingly frustrated and was on the verge of giving up when he had an idea.

One day, while taking a break from his work, Farny picked up a newspaper and read an article about a toy called "silly putty." The article described how silly putty was a stretchy, bouncy substance made from silicone, and Farny immediately realized that this could be the solution to his problem.

Farny went to a toy store and bought a few containers of silly putty. He then mixed the silicone rubber in a beaker and poured it onto the silly putty, which he had stretched out to the desired size. To his amazement, the silicone rubber stuck to the silly putty and formed a perfect sheet. Farny had solved the problem that had stumped Dow Chemical for months.

Farny's discovery was a breakthrough that changed the field of materials science. He had found a way to make large sheets of silicone rubber, which could be used in a wide range of applications, from aerospace to medical devices. Farny's success was not only due to his technical expertise but also his determination to find a solution to the problem. He was willing to try unconventional methods and to think outside the box, which led to his breakthrough.

The story of James Farny and his use of silly putty as a mold for silicone rubber is a great example of how determination, persistence, and creativity can lead to success. Farny was faced with a seemingly impossible problem, but he never gave up. He was willing to try unconventional methods and to think outside the box, which ultimately led to his breakthrough discovery.

"The bad news is time flies. The good news is you're the pilot." - Michael Altshuler

Eugene Cernan

Eugene Cernan's experience on the moon is a poignant illustration of how quickly time can pass and how important it is to take control of our lives. As an astronaut, Cernan had achieved the pinnacle of his career by becoming the last person to walk on the moon. However, during his mission, he had a moment of profound realization that would stay with him for the rest of his life.

Cernan was standing on the lunar surface, looking back at Earth, when he had a sudden realization. He said, "I was never able to see tomorrow, but I could always remember yesterday. And I realized, when I was looking back at the Earth, that if I don't go back, if I don't get in that spacecraft and come home, I'm going to miss tomorrow. I'm going to miss the rest of my life."

At that moment, Cernan realized how quickly time passes and how important it is to make the most of every moment. He understood that he was the pilot of his own life and that he needed to take control of his future. He knew that if he didn't seize the moment and make the most of his life, he would miss out on the things that were most important to him.

This experience had a profound impact on Cernan, and he became an advocate for living life to the fullest. He believed that we all have the power to control our own destiny and make the most of the time we have. He urged people to take risks, pursue their passions, and never let fear hold them back.

Eugene Cernan's experience on the moon is a powerful reminder that time flies and we are the pilots of our own lives. We need to be intentional about how we spend our time and make the most of every moment, so that we don't miss out on the things that are most important to us.

"Keep your face always toward the sunshine, and shadows will fall behind you." - Walt Whitman

Diana Nyad

Diana Nyad began her swimming career as a teenager and quickly established herself as a talented long-distance swimmer. In 1978, at the age of 28, she attempted to swim from Cuba to Florida for the first time, but her attempt was thwarted by strong currents, high waves, and a shark attack. Nyad made several more attempts over the next three decades, but each time she was forced to abandon her swim due to various obstacles, including asthma, hypothermia, and severe jellyfish stings.

Despite these setbacks, Nyad remained determined to achieve her goal of swimming from Cuba to Florida, and in 2013, at the age of 64, she made her fifth and final attempt. She was accompanied by a team of support boats, but she did not use a shark cage, as this would have disqualified her from the official record. Nyad swam for 53 hours straight, covering 110 miles in total, and battled through adverse weather conditions, jellyfish stings, and extreme exhaustion.

During the entire swim, Nyad maintained a steadfast gaze towards the sun, tapping into her inner reservoirs of fortitude and determination to overcome the physical discomfort and mental uncertainty. She used mental visualization techniques, recited poetry to herself, and focused on her breathing and stroke to maintain her momentum and keep her mind calm. When she finally emerged from the water on the shores of Florida, Nyad was exhausted but elated, having achieved her lifelong dream and set a new record for the longest ocean swim without a shark cage.

Nyad's story is a powerful example of the importance of perseverance and resilience in the face of adversity. By staying positive and focused on her goal, even in the midst of multiple failures and setbacks, she was able to achieve something that many people thought was impossible. Her determination and bravery continue to inspire people around the world to pursue their own dreams, no matter how difficult or unlikely they may seem.

"Life has got all those twists and turns. You've got to hold on tight and off you go." - Nicole Kidman

Mark Cuban

After graduating from college with a degree in computer science, Mark Cuban moved to Dallas, Texas, to start his career. However, he soon discovered that finding a job in his field was not as easy as he thought. Despite his impressive qualifications, he struggled to find work, and he was forced to take a job as a bartender to make ends meet.

Even though Cuban was disheartened by the lack of job opportunities in his preferred profession, he persisted in pursuing his ambition of becoming a thriving entrepreneur. He used his time working as a bartender to learn about business and customer service, and he eventually started his own company, MicroSolutions, which provided computer consulting services to businesses in the Dallas area.

Cuban's experience working as a bartender taught him the importance of customer service, and he used this knowledge to build a successful business. MicroSolutions grew quickly, and Cuban eventually sold the company for millions of dollars. This success allowed him to start his own investment company, which he used to invest in a variety of successful startups.

However, Cuban's journey to success was not always smooth sailing. He experienced a number of setbacks and failures along the way, including the failure of his first business venture, a software company called Your Business Software. Despite these setbacks, Cuban did not give up on his dream of being a successful entrepreneur. He continued to take risks and embrace new opportunities, and this eventually led him to co-found Broadcast.com, which he sold to Yahoo! for almost $6 billion.

Today, Cuban is a well-known investor and owner of the NBA's Dallas Mavericks. He has also become known for his appearances on the television show Shark Tank, where he offers advice and investments to up-and-coming entrepreneurs. Across his professional journey, Cuban has stressed the significance of flexibility and welcoming transformation as key ingredients for attaining prosperity.. He believes that the most successful people are the ones who are able to adapt to changing circumstances and take advantage of unexpected opportunities. This attitude has served him well over the years, and it continues to inspire others to pursue their own dreams, even in the face of adversity.

"You make a choice: continue living your life feeling muddled in this abyss of self-misunderstanding, or you find your identity independent of it. You draw your own box." - Duchess Meghan

Oprah Winfrey

Mississippi saw the arrival of Oprah Winfrey in 1954, who encountered a trying upbringing defined by destitution, maltreatment, and prejudice Despite these challenges, she was a gifted student and began working in media as a teenager, eventually landing her own radio show while still in high school.

In the 1980s, Oprah began hosting a morning talk show in Chicago, which soon became wildly popular. However, early on in her career, she was told that she needed to conform to certain standards of appearance and demeanor in order to be successful. For example, she was advised to lose weight, straighten her hair, and adopt a more traditional, "neutral" approach to her interviews.

Instead of following this advice, Oprah decided to be true to herself and her unique perspective. She embraced her natural appearance, including her curly hair, and began to use her platform to talk about issues that were important to her, including social justice, mental health, and personal growth. She also started incorporating more emotional and personal elements into her interviews, encouraging her guests to open up and share their own stories.

Over time, Oprah's authenticity and willingness to be vulnerable on camera endeared her to millions of viewers. She became one of the most successful talk show hosts of all time, eventually launching her own media company, Harpo Productions, and creating a hugely popular book club and magazine. In addition, she has used her wealth and influence to support a range of philanthropic causes, including education, health, and social justice.

Oprah has consistently championed the notion that true success is not derived from adhering to societal norms and standards, but rather from embracing one's own distinctive identity and viewpoint. This has been a recurring theme throughout her professional journey. She has said, "I had no idea that being your authentic self could make me as rich as I've become. If I had, I'd have done it a lot earlier." By drawing her own box and staying true to herself, Oprah has achieved extraordinary success and become a role model for people around the world.

"Be courageous. Challenge orthodoxy. Stand up for what you believe in. When you are in your rocking chair talking to your grandchildren many years from now, be sure you have a good story to tell." - Amal Clooney

Malala Yousafzai

On July 12, 1997, Malala made her entrance into the world in Mingora, a city situated in the Swat Valley area of Pakistan. Her father, Ziauddin Yousafzai, was a teacher and an activist who ran a school for girls in their hometown. Malala was inspired by her father's work and from a young age, she was an advocate for girls' education.

However, in 2009, the Taliban took control of Swat Valley and banned girls from attending school. Malala was just 11 years old at the time, but she refused to be silenced. She began writing a blog for the BBC, under a pseudonym, about the difficulties of being a girl who wanted an education under the Taliban's rule.

As Malala's profile grew, she became a target of the Taliban. On October 9, 2012, as she was on her way home from school, a Taliban gunman boarded her school bus and shot her in the head. She was airlifted to a hospital in the UK, where she underwent multiple surgeries and made a remarkable recovery.

After her recovery, Malala became an even more prominent activist for girls' education. She continued to speak out and advocate for education, even as the Taliban threatened her and her family. In 2014, at the age of 17, she became the youngest-ever Nobel Prize laureate, sharing the award with Indian children's rights activist Kailash Satyarthi.

Since then, Malala has continued to advocate for girls' education around the world. She has spoken at the United Nations and started the Malala Fund, which works to ensure that every girl has access to 12 years of free, safe, and quality education. She has also written several books, including an autobiography, "I Am Malala," which has been translated into more than 40 languages.

Malala's narrative serves as a compelling testament to the fact that, despite encountering hostility and brutality, we can remain resolute in our convictions and actively strive for progress. She is a role model for young people around the world, and her courage and determination continue to inspire millions of people to work towards a more just and equitable world.

"You are never too old to set another goal or to dream a new dream." - Malala Yousafzai

Anna Mary Robertson Moses

Born in 1860 in upstate New York, Anna Mary Robertson Moses spent the majority of her life engaged in farming and raising a family. She married at the age of 27 and had ten children, five of whom survived into adulthood. Throughout her life, Moses enjoyed making crafts and quilts, and would often create her own designs.

In the winter of 1936, when Moses was 76 years old, she was no longer able to do embroidery due to arthritis. Looking for a new creative outlet, she picked up a paintbrush for the first time. She began painting scenes of rural life and the landscapes of her home state, often from memory. She used bright colors and bold outlines to capture the simplicity and charm of rural America.

Moses' paintings caught the attention of a New York art collector named Louis Caldor, who discovered her work while visiting the town of Hoosick Falls. Caldor was impressed by Moses' paintings and brought them to the attention of a New York City art gallery.

In 1940, at the age of 80, Moses had her first solo exhibition at the Galerie St. Etienne in New York City. Her paintings were an instant success, with many selling for hundreds of dollars. She quickly gained recognition for her unique style and her ability to capture the spirit of rural America.

Over the next several years, Moses continued to paint and exhibit her work. She became one of the most famous artists in the United States, and her paintings were featured in galleries and museums across the country. She was even commissioned to create a painting for President Harry Truman's birthday in 1951.

Throughout her career, Moses remained humble and down-to-earth, often referring to herself as "just a plain old lady." She continued to paint until her death in 1961, at the age of 101.

Grandma Moses' success as an artist is a testament to the fact that it is never too late to pursue your passions and achieve your dreams. Despite starting her artistic career at an age when most people are winding down, she was able to find success and recognition for her work, and her legacy continues to inspire artists of all ages to this day.

"I just want you to know that if you are out there and you are being really hard on yourself right now for something that has happened ... it's normal. That is what is going to happen to you in life. No one gets through unscathed. We are all going to have a few scratches on us. Please be kind to yourselves and stand up for yourself, please." - Taylor Swift

Dwayne "The Rock" Johnson

Dwayne Johnson's journey to success was not an easy one. He was born into a family of professional wrestlers and grew up with the dream of following in their footsteps. After playing college football, he pursued a career in the NFL but was ultimately cut from the Calgary Stampeders in 1995. This was a major setback for him, as he had invested a lot of time and effort into pursuing a career in football.

Following his release from the CFL, Johnson fell into a deep depression. He had to move back in with his parents, and he felt like a failure. He was struggling to find his place in the world, and he felt like he had let his family down.

Despite his depression, Johnson knew he needed to keep pushing forward. He started training harder and began looking for other opportunities to pursue. That's when he decided to follow in his family's footsteps and pursue a career in professional wrestling.

He started off in small wrestling circuits, but his talent and charisma quickly caught the attention of bigger wrestling companies. Eventually, he landed a contract with the World Wrestling Federation (now known as WWE) and became one of the biggest stars in the industry.

But even as his career took off, Johnson continued to struggle with depression. In a 2018 interview with Express UK, he said, "Struggle and pain is real. I was devastated and depressed. I reached a point where I didn't want to do a thing or go anywhere. I was crying constantly."

Undeterred by the challenges he faced, Johnson persisted and dedicated himself to his aspirations, ultimately making the transition from wrestling to acting. He has since become one of the most successful actors in Hollywood, starring in blockbuster films like the Fast and Furious franchise and Jumanji.

Johnson has maintained a policy of transparency regarding his battles with depression, utilizing his influence to urge individuals who may be undergoing comparable ordeals to pursue assistance. He has said, "Depression never discriminates. Took me a long time to realize it but the key is to not be afraid to open up. Especially us dudes have a tendency to keep it in. You're not alone."

Johnson's story is a powerful reminder that even the most successful people face challenges and setbacks, and that it's important to be kind to yourself and seek help when you need it.

"People tell you the world looks a certain way. Parents tell you how to think. Schools tell you how to think. TV. Religion. And then at a certain point, if you're lucky, you realize you can make up your own mind. Nobody sets the rules but you. You can design your own life." - Carrie Ann Moss

Richard Branson

Born in 1950 in England, Richard Branson encountered academic challenges in school, largely due to his dyslexia, but his entrepreneurial spirit persisted throughout. When he was 17, he started a magazine called "Student" with some of his friends. The magazine covered topics that were of interest to young people, such as music and fashion.

The magazine was a success and Branson used the contacts he made through the magazine to start a mail-order record business. He called the business Virgin Records, because he and his business partners felt like they were new to the music industry.

Virgin Records started small, with Branson selling records out of the trunk of his car. But he quickly expanded the business and opened a record shop in London. Virgin Records became known for signing new and innovative artists, such as the Sex Pistols and the Rolling Stones.

In the 1980s, Branson expanded his business empire to include airlines, trains, and telecommunications. His most notable venture was Virgin Atlantic Airways, which he launched in 1984. Branson started the airline to challenge the established airlines like British Airways, which he felt were not serving customers well.

Branson overcame numerous obstacles and naysayers to tenaciously pursue his entrepreneurial ambitions. He did not let his struggles in school or other people's expectations limit him. He followed his own instincts and passions, and was able to design his own life and build a successful business empire.

Today, Richard Branson is one of the most successful entrepreneurs in the world, with a net worth of over $4 billion. His story illustrates how it's possible to succeed in life by thinking outside the box and pursuing one's own vision, even in the face of adversity.

"At the end of the day, whether or not those people are comfortable with how you're living your life doesn't matter. What matters is whether you're comfortable with it." - Dr. Phil

Emma Watson

In 2014, actress Emma Watson was named a UN Women Goodwill Ambassador, a role that tasked her with promoting gender equality and women's rights on a global scale. Watson had become a household name thanks to her role as Hermione Granger in the Harry Potter films, but she had also been involved in advocacy work for several years, including serving as an ambassador for Camfed, a charity that works to educate girls in sub-Saharan Africa.

Despite Watson's previous involvement in advocacy work, her appointment as a UN Women Goodwill Ambassador was met with a lot of criticism and backlash. Many people questioned her qualifications and experience, and some accused her of being a "feminist fake" or simply seeking attention.

Watson could have easily let the criticism get to her and backed away from the role, but she didn't. Instead, she used the platform to advocate for women's rights and raise awareness about important issues. She made a powerful speech at the UN in which she urged men to join the fight for gender equality, and she launched the HeForShe campaign, which calls on men to support women's rights and gender equality.

Watson's work as a UN Women Goodwill Ambassador has been widely praised, and she has become a respected advocate in the field. She has continued to speak out about issues like sexual harassment and assault, and has used her platform to elevate the voices of marginalized groups.

Through it all, Watson has remained true to herself and her values. She recognized that what mattered most was whether she was comfortable with her actions and whether they aligned with her beliefs and values. She refused to let the opinions of others dictate how she lived her life, and in doing so, she has made a positive impact on the world and inspired others to do the same.

"Do not allow people to dim your shine because they are blinded. Tell them to put some sunglasses on." - Lady Gaga

Maya Angelou

In the 1950s, Maya Angelou was working as a dancer in a nightclub in Rome, Italy. One night, after a particularly energetic performance, Maya overheard some members of the audience making disparaging comments about her dancing. They were surprised that a black woman could dance so gracefully and with such skill.

Instead of letting their comments bring her down, Maya decided to confront them. She walked over to their table and said, "You know, it's funny you should say that. Because I've been working on the art of dance for 25 years, and I think I'm pretty good. But if you don't like the way I dance, that's okay. Just remember, I didn't come here to dance for you. I came here to dance for me."

Maya's response was powerful because it showed that she was not willing to let anyone else's opinions diminish her sense of self-worth or her love of her craft. She had worked hard to hone her skills as a dancer, and she was proud of what she had accomplished. Even though the audience members were trying to bring her down, Maya refused to let them dim her shine.

This anecdote is a great example of what Lady Gaga meant when she said, "Do not allow people to dim your shine because they are blinded. Tell them to put some sunglasses on." Maya was a shining example of resilience and self-confidence, refusing to let anyone else's negativity or ignorance bring her down. Instead, she chose to embrace her own light and shine as brightly as she could, regardless of what others might say.

"Spread love everywhere you go." - Mother Teresa

Fred Rogers

Fred Rogers was the creator and host of the popular children's television program, "Mister Rogers' Neighborhood," which aired from 1968 to 2001. Over the course of his career, he became known for his gentle, compassionate, and empathetic approach to teaching children about the world around them.

One day, while speaking to a group of children, Mr. Rogers was asked about recent events in the news. The children were concerned about things like war, violence, and other troubling issues, and didn't know what they could do to help.

In response, Mr. Rogers encouraged the children to spread love and kindness wherever they went. He told them, "There are three ways to ultimate success: The first way is to be kind. The second way is to be kind. The third way is to be kind."

He went on to explain that even small acts of kindness can make a big difference in the world. He said, "Imagine what our real neighborhoods would be like if each of us offered, as a matter of course, just one kind word to another person... One kind word has a wonderful way of turning into many."

Mr. Rogers' message of spreading love and kindness resonated with generations of children and adults alike. His approach to teaching and his unwavering commitment to the power of love and compassion have become part of his lasting legacy. Today, people continue to be inspired by his example and strive to make the world a more loving and compassionate place.

"If you make your internal life a priority, then everything else you need on the outside will be given to you and it will be extremely clear what the next step is." - Gabrielle Bernstein

Marianne Williamson

In the early 1980s, Williamson was a struggling actress living in New York City. She was deeply unhappy with her life and felt unfulfilled in her acting career. She began to explore different spiritual teachings and practices, looking for a way to find meaning and purpose in her life.

Eventually, she discovered the teachings of A Course in Miracles, a spiritual text that would have a profound impact on her life. The principles of love, forgiveness, and spiritual transformation resonated deeply with her, and she began to apply them to her own life.

Williamson started teaching the principles of A Course in Miracles to small groups of people in her living room. As she continued to focus on her internal growth and spiritual development, her teachings began to attract larger and larger audiences. People were drawn to her message of love and forgiveness, and her workshops and lectures became popular around the country.

As her popularity grew, Williamson began to write books about her spiritual teachings. In 1992, she published "A Return to Love," a book that combined the teachings of A Course in Miracles with her own personal experiences and insights. The book became a bestseller, selling over three million copies and being translated into 27 languages.

Williamson's message of love and forgiveness also began to have an impact outside of the spiritual community. She became involved in social and political activism, advocating for causes such as AIDS awareness, poverty reduction, and peace in the Middle East. In 2014, she ran for Congress in California's 33rd district, advocating for a more compassionate and loving approach to politics.

Throughout her journey, Williamson has remained committed to her spiritual practice and to making her internal life a priority. She has continued to teach and write about the principles of love, forgiveness, and spiritual transformation, and has inspired countless people around the world to live more fulfilling and meaningful lives.

"You can be everything. You can be the infinite amount of things that people are." – Kesha

Misty Copeland

Misty Copeland is an accomplished ballerina who has made a significant impact in the world of ballet. Born in 1982, Copeland grew up in San Pedro, California. She was introduced to ballet at the age of 13 through a free program at her local Boys & Girls Club. Despite starting relatively late in her training, Copeland's natural talent and dedication quickly became evident.

In 1998, Copeland joined the American Ballet Theatre's Studio Company, a pre-professional program that serves as a stepping stone to the main company. She was promoted to the corps de ballet, the lowest rank of professional dancers, in 2001. Over the next few years, Copeland continued to climb the ranks, earning soloist status in 2007 and then becoming a principal dancer in 2015.

Copeland's promotion to principal dancer made history, as she became the first African American woman to hold the position at the American Ballet Theatre. Her achievement was widely celebrated as a significant step forward in the quest for greater diversity and inclusion in the world of ballet.

Copeland's story is one of perseverance and dedication. She faced numerous challenges in her career, including several serious injuries that threatened to end her dancing days. However, she never gave up, always pushing herself to be the best dancer she could be.

In addition to her impressive accomplishments as a ballerina, Copeland has also become a powerful voice for change in the world of dance. She has been an outspoken advocate for diversity and inclusion, using her platform to inspire young dancers, particularly those from underrepresented communities, to pursue their dreams.

Through her talent, hard work, and dedication, Misty Copeland has become a shining example of what can be achieved when one sets their mind to it. Her story is a reminder that anyone can be anything they want to be, regardless of their background or circumstances.

"You don't always need a plan. Sometimes you just need to breathe, trust, let go and see what happens." - Mandy Hale

Jack Dorsey

In the early 2000s, Jack Dorsey was working as a programmer in Silicon Valley. One of the projects he was working on was a system for dispatching emergency services to the right locations. As part of this project, he started to notice that people were using SMS to send updates to their friends and family about what they were doing and where they were.

Dorsey had the idea to take this concept of short, status updates and turn it into a platform for broadcasting messages to a large number of people at once. He started working on a prototype for the platform, which he called "twttr" (a name inspired by the fact that it used SMS messages, which were limited to 160 characters).

Dorsey showed the prototype to a few friends and colleagues, and they liked it. He continued to work on the platform, building out its features and capabilities. In March 2006, the first version of Twitter was launched.

At first, Twitter didn't have a clear business model or revenue stream. Dorsey and his team were focused on building a product that people would find useful and engaging. The platform gained popularity quickly, with users using it to share news, thoughts, and experiences with their followers.

However, Twitter also faced challenges in its early years. The platform experienced frequent outages and technical issues, and there were concerns about how it could be monetized. Dorsey stepped down as CEO in 2008, but remained involved with the company as chairman of the board.

Despite these challenges, Twitter continued to grow and evolve. The platform added new features, such as the ability to include photos and videos in tweets, and expanded its reach to new markets around the world. Twitter also found ways to monetize the platform, through advertising and partnerships with other companies.

Today, Twitter is one of the most widely used social media platforms in the world, with millions of users and a market value of over $40 billion. Jack Dorsey's story illustrates the power of having a good idea and the willingness to take a risk, even if you don't have a detailed plan or clear path to success. By breathing, trusting, and letting go, Dorsey was able to create a platform that has had a profound impact on how we communicate and connect with each other.

"I want to be in the arena. I want to be brave with my life. And when we make the choice to dare greatly, we sign up to get our asses kicked. We can choose courage or we can choose comfort, but we can't have both. Not at the same time." - Brene Brown

Arthur Ashe

Arthur Ashe was born in 1943 in Richmond, Virginia, and grew up during a time when racial segregation was still widespread in the United States. Despite facing discrimination and racism throughout his life, Ashe was an exceptional athlete and went on to become one of the greatest tennis players of his generation.

Ashe's career was marked by numerous accomplishments, including three Grand Slam titles and his historic victory at Wimbledon in 1975. But Ashe was also known for his activism and advocacy, particularly around issues of social justice and equality.

During his lifetime, Ashe utilized his platform to advocate for causes such as racial discrimination, apartheid in South Africa, and the imperative for enhanced accessibility to education and healthcare. He was an advocate for the underprivileged and marginalized, and was particularly committed to using sports as a means of promoting social change.

In 1983, Ashe was diagnosed with HIV, which at the time was a relatively unknown and highly stigmatized disease. Rather than retreat from public life or hide his illness, Ashe chose to use his platform to raise awareness and fight against the discrimination that people with AIDS were facing.

Ashe knew that speaking out about AIDS would be a difficult and potentially dangerous task, given the level of stigma and misinformation surrounding the disease. But he believed that it was important to use his voice to educate people and advocate for change.

Ashe's decision to come forward about his illness was met with a mixed response from the public. Some praised him for his bravery and admired his commitment to raising awareness about AIDS. Others, however, were critical of Ashe and his decision to speak out, and he faced significant backlash from some quarters.

In spite of the obstacles he encountered, Ashe persisted in utilizing his voice and platform to advocate for increased comprehension and empathy regarding AIDS. He spoke out about the need for more funding for AIDS research and education, and worked to dispel myths and misconceptions about the disease.

Ashe passed away from AIDS-related complications in 1993, but his legacy as a courageous athlete and advocate for social justice lives on. His life and work serve as a powerful example of what it means to choose courage over comfort, and to use our talents and resources to make a positive impact on the world

"I'm going to be gone one day, and I have to accept that tomorrow isn't promised. Am I OK with how I'm living today? It's the only thing I can help. If I didn't have another one, what have I done with all my todays? Am I doing a good job?" - Hayley Williams

Chadwick Boseman

Chadwick Boseman's speech at Howard University's 2018 commencement ceremony was not only inspiring, but also poignant, given that the actor was privately battling colon cancer at the time. Despite his illness, he delivered a powerful message to the graduates about the importance of living a purposeful life.

During the speech, Boseman emphasized the need to pursue one's passions and to work hard to achieve one's goals. He also spoke about the value of failure, and how it can lead to growth and success in the long run. He said, "When you are deciding on next steps, next jobs, next careers, further education, you should rather find purpose than a job or a career. Purpose crosses disciplines. Purpose is an essential element of you."

Boseman's message was particularly meaningful given his own experiences. He had been diagnosed with colon cancer in 2016, but had kept his illness private while he continued to work and create. During this time, he delivered some of his most memorable performances, including his portrayal of T'Challa/Black Panther in the Marvel Cinematic Universe.

In fact, Boseman's work on Black Panther was a shining example of his commitment to using his platform for social justice causes. The film was a cultural phenomenon, celebrating Black excellence and challenging traditional Hollywood narratives. Boseman used his platform to advocate for greater representation and inclusion in the film industry, and to shine a light on issues like police brutality and racial inequality.

Sadly, Boseman passed away in 2020, at the age of 43. His death came as a shock to many, as he had kept his illness private and had continued to work on projects until shortly before his passing. But even in death, his legacy lives on. He inspired countless people with his words and actions, and his dedication to using his talents to make a difference in the world will be remembered for years to come.

"Belief creates the actual fact." - William James

Colonel Sanders

Born in 1890 in Henryville, Indiana, Colonel Sanders had a challenging upbringing, with the loss of both his parents by the time he was merely ten years old. He was forced to drop out of school and take on odd jobs to help support himself and his siblings.

Over the years, Sanders held a variety of jobs, including farmhand, streetcar conductor, and insurance salesman. He even served in the U.S. Army during World War I.

In 1929, Sanders opened a gas station in Corbin, Kentucky. He also started cooking and selling his own recipe for fried chicken to travelers passing through. The recipe quickly gained a reputation for being delicious, and Sanders began to attract more and more customers.

Notwithstanding the triumph of his chicken recipe, Sanders confronted multiple challenges when endeavoring to pitch his formula to eateries. He traveled across the country, pitching his recipe to countless restaurant owners, but he was rejected time and time again.

But despite the rejection, Sanders never lost faith in his product. He believed that his chicken was the best out there, and he was determined to find a way to share it with the world.

It wasn't until Sanders was in his 60s that he finally found success. In 1952, he franchised his recipe and opened the first Kentucky Fried Chicken restaurant in Salt Lake City, Utah. From there, the business took off, and KFC became a worldwide phenomenon.

Colonel Sanders' story underscores the criticality of self-belief in accomplishing success. Even though he encountered multiple obstacles and setbacks, he persevered with unrelenting faith in himself and his product. He believed that his chicken was the best out there, and he was determined to find a way to share it with the world. And in the end, that belief paid off in the form of a successful business that has lasted for generations.

"No matter what people tell you, words and ideas can change the world." - Robin Williams as John Keating in Dead Poets Society

Ron Stallworth

Ron Stallworth's story begins in 1972 when he joined the Colorado Springs police department as its first black officer. Two years later, he was working in the intelligence unit when he saw an ad in the local newspaper for the Ku Klux Klan. Curious, he decided to call the number listed in the ad, pretending to be a white supremacist interested in joining the organization.

Over the phone, Stallworth was able to convince the KKK members that he was white and shared their hateful ideology. He even had a few conversations with David Duke, the Grand Wizard of the KKK at the time. But Stallworth knew that he could not attend any KKK meetings in person because of his race. So, he came up with a plan to send a white police officer in his place.

Stallworth recruited his colleague, Flip Zimmerman, to play the part of "Ron Stallworth" in person. Zimmerman had to attend several KKK meetings, including one where he had to take a polygraph test to prove his loyalty to the organization. The KKK members were suspicious of Zimmerman at first, but eventually, they accepted him as one of their own.

While Zimmerman was attending KKK meetings, Stallworth was gathering intelligence on the group through phone conversations with other members. Their efforts led to the arrest and conviction of several KKK members for various crimes, including attempted murder.

Stallworth chronicled his experience in a book called "Black Klansman," which was later adapted into a feature film by Spike Lee. The film, also called "Black Klansman," was released in 2018 and received critical acclaim, including an Academy Award for Best Adapted Screenplay.

Through his work as an undercover police officer, Stallworth was able to use his words and ideas to challenge the hateful and bigoted ideology of the KKK, ultimately contributing to positive change in his community. His story is a powerful example of how words and ideas can be used to combat hate and intolerance.

"It is during our darkest moments that we must focus to see the light."- Aristotle

Nick Vujicic

Nick Vujicic came into the world on December 4, 1982, in Melbourne, Australia, with tetra-amelia syndrome, an uncommon ailment that deprived him of both arms and legs. His parents were shocked and devastated by the news, and Nick faced countless physical and emotional challenges growing up.

As a child, Nick was bullied and felt like an outcast. He struggled with depression and thoughts of suicide, wondering why he was born the way he was and what purpose his life could have. But in his teenage years, Nick discovered a new sense of purpose when he became a Christian. He found hope and meaning in his faith and realized that he could use his unique story to inspire and motivate others.

Nick began giving motivational speeches as a teenager, sharing his story of overcoming obstacles and finding joy and purpose in life. He founded his own non-profit organization, Life Without Limbs, to provide support and encouragement to people around the world who are facing challenges and adversity. Nick's message of hope and perseverance resonated with people of all ages and backgrounds, and he soon became a sought-after speaker and author.

Over the years, Nick has traveled to over 60 countries, speaking to millions of people and spreading his message of hope and inspiration. He has written several books, including "Life Without Limits: Inspiration for a Ridiculously Good Life" and "Unstoppable: The Incredible Power of Faith in Action." He has also been featured on numerous television shows and in documentaries, and has received many awards and honors for his work.

Today, Nick is happily married and a father of four children. He continues to inspire and motivate people around the world with his message of hope and positivity. Despite facing countless obstacles and challenges in his life, Nick has found a way to focus on what he can do, rather than what he can't, and his story is a testament to the power of resilience and determination in the face of adversity.

"I'm not going to continue knocking that old door that doesn't open for me. I'm going to create my own door and walk through that." - Ava DuVernay

Gina Rodriguez

Gina Rodriguez was born and raised in Chicago, Illinois, and grew up with a passion for acting. After studying at the Tisch School of the Arts at New York University, she moved to Los Angeles to pursue a career in Hollywood.

However, despite her talent, Rodriguez found that opportunities for Latina actresses in Hollywood were limited, and she was often told that she wasn't "Latina enough" or "not white enough" for certain roles. She struggled to find work and was on the verge of giving up on her dream.

But instead of giving up, Rodriguez decided to take matters into her own hands. She started her own production company, I Can and I Will Productions, and produced and starred in the independent film "Filly Brown," a drama about a young Latina rapper trying to make it in the music industry.

The film premiered at the 2012 Sundance Film Festival, where it earned critical acclaim and was hailed as a breakthrough for Latinx representation in Hollywood. The success of "Filly Brown" helped Rodriguez to secure more opportunities in the industry, and she went on to land her breakthrough role in the hit TV show "Jane the Virgin."

Since then, Rodriguez has continued to use her platform to advocate for diversity and representation in the entertainment industry. She has spoken out about the importance of including underrepresented voices in film and television, and has produced and starred in projects that showcase the experiences of marginalized communities.

Through her perseverance and determination, Gina Rodriguez has created her own opportunities and made a name for herself in an industry that often overlooks people of color. Her story serves as an inspiration to anyone who has faced obstacles in pursuing their dreams, and a reminder that sometimes the best way to succeed is to create your own path.

"Not having the best situation, but seeing the best in your situation is the key to happiness." - Marie Forleo

Tatyana McFadden

Due to spina bifida, a congenital anomaly that resulted in her spinal cord being exposed at birth, Tatyana McFadden became paralyzed from the waist down. She spent the first six years of her life in a Russian orphanage, where she was forced to walk on her hands because there were no wheelchairs available. In 1994, she was adopted by Deborah McFadden, an American woman who was working as the commissioner of disabilities in the U.S. Department of Health and Human Services.

Deborah McFadden helped Tatyana get the medical care and equipment she needed to thrive. She also encouraged her daughter to pursue sports, which Tatyana began participating in during high school. She quickly discovered that she had a talent for athletics, and went on to become one of the most accomplished Paralympic athletes of all time.

Tatyana has won 17 Paralympic medals in track and field and cross-country skiing, and has also won multiple marathons and road races. In 2013, she won the women's wheelchair race at the Boston Marathon, just one week after winning the women's wheelchair race at the London Marathon. She has also competed in the New York City Marathon, the Chicago Marathon, and the Berlin Marathon.

Tatyana has managed to sustain a positive outlook on life in the face of daunting challenges. In an interview with the New York Times, she said, "I think it's really important to focus on the positives in life, and not dwell on the negatives. I've had some tough times, but I try to stay positive and keep pushing forward."

Tatyana's narrative provides a compelling demonstration of how a constructive demeanor and an unwavering commitment to concentrating on life's blessings can enable us to surmount even the most formidable obstacles. By refusing to let her disability define her, Tatyana has achieved extraordinary success and inspired countless others to do the same.

"Just don't give up trying to do what you really want to do. Where there is love and inspiration, I don't think you can go wrong." - Ella Fitzgerald

Jack Ma

Jack Ma's journey to success began in the 1990s when he first learned about the internet while on a business trip to the United States. At the time, he was working as an English teacher in China and had no prior experience in technology or business.

Despite his lack of expertise, Ma became fascinated with the potential of the internet and began learning everything he could about it. He spent countless hours in internet cafes, reading books and manuals, and practicing his programming skills.

In 1995, Ma founded China Pages, a website that aimed to connect Chinese businesses with customers around the world. However, the venture was not successful, and the company struggled to attract customers and generate revenue.

Undeterred, Ma continued to believe in his vision of helping small businesses in China to connect with the rest of the world. In 1999, he founded Alibaba, an online marketplace that allowed Chinese businesses to sell their products to customers around the globe.

At first, Alibaba faced many challenges. There were few online shoppers in China at the time, and the company struggled to compete with established e-commerce giants like eBay. However, Ma and his team persisted, building a reputation for honesty and reliability and emphasizing the importance of customer service.

Over time, Alibaba became the go-to platform for small and medium-sized businesses in China, and the company's success continued to grow. Today, Alibaba is one of the world's largest e-commerce companies, with a market capitalization of over $600 billion.

During the course of his career, Jack Ma has underscored the significance of perseverance, vision, and an ardent enthusiasm for one's occupation. His story is a powerful example of what can be achieved through hard work, determination, and a willingness to take risks and follow one's dreams.

"Weaknesses are just strengths in the wrong environment." - Marianne Cantwell

Chris Gardner

Chris Gardner was born in Milwaukee, Wisconsin, in 1954, and his early life was marked by poverty, abuse, and academic struggles. His mother, Bettye Jean Triplett, was unable to support him and his siblings, and Gardner's abusive stepfather made their home life even more difficult. Gardner's struggles continued into his academic life, as he was unable to read due to undiagnosed dyslexia.

Despite these challenges, Gardner refused to give up on his dreams of success. After serving in the Navy, he moved to San Francisco and began working as a medical equipment salesman. However, he struggled to make ends meet and was often unable to pay his rent. He eventually became homeless, and at one point, he even had to spend the night in a public restroom.

One day, while he was homeless and sleeping in a public restroom, Gardner saw a man driving a red Ferrari and asked him what he did for a living. The man said he was a stockbroker, which inspired Gardner to pursue a career in finance. He applied for an internship at a stock brokerage firm called Dean Witter Reynolds, but he faced numerous challenges there as well. He was the only African-American in the program, and he struggled with the fast-paced and competitive environment.

However, Gardner refused to give up. He used his innate resilience and determination to overcome his weaknesses, working hard to learn the ropes of the finance industry. Despite facing numerous setbacks and challenges, Gardner succeeded in the program and went on to become a successful stockbroker and entrepreneur.

Today, Gardner is a sought-after motivational speaker and philanthropist, known for his inspiring message of perseverance and the idea that weaknesses can be transformed into strengths in the right environment. He has also founded several organizations aimed at helping the homeless and the underprivileged, including the Chris Gardner Foundation and the Happyness Foundation.

"Silence is the last thing the world will ever hear from me." - Marlee Matlin

Mae Jemison

Mae Jemison is a physician and former NASA astronaut who became the first African American woman to travel to space. Born on October 17, 1956, in Decatur, Alabama, Jemison was raised in Chicago, Illinois, where she developed an early interest in science and space exploration. She was inspired by the historic moon landing in 1969, which occurred when she was just 12 years old.

Jemison excelled in school and went on to attend Stanford University, where she earned a degree in chemical engineering in 1977. She then pursued a medical degree at Cornell University, and graduated in 1981. Jemison completed her residency at the Los Angeles County-USC Medical Center, and worked as a general practitioner before applying to NASA's astronaut program.

Jemison was one of 15 candidates selected by NASA in 1987 for its astronaut training program. After a year of rigorous training, she was selected to serve on the Space Shuttle Endeavour crew for mission STS-47 in 1992. During her time in space, Jemison conducted experiments on motion sickness and bone cell research, and also carried out the first successful test of an autonomous medical diagnosis system.

Following her historic flight, Jemison left NASA and went on to pursue a wide range of interests. She founded The Jemison Group, a company focused on technology and social issues, and has also served as a professor of environmental studies at Dartmouth College. She is a strong advocate for science education and diversity, and has been recognized for her efforts with numerous awards and honors.

Jemison's career has been a living embodiment of the maxim "Silence is the last thing the world will ever hear from me." Through her voice and accomplishments, she has spurred and encouraged others and remains an exemplar for young people globally.

"Learning how to be still, to really be still and let life happen—that stillness becomes a radiance." - Morgan Freeman

Ludovico Einaudi

Ludovico Einaudi is an Italian pianist and composer known for his minimalist and ambient music. He has released over 20 albums and collaborated with various artists throughout his career. However, Einaudi's journey to success was not without its challenges.

Early in his career, Einaudi suffered from stage fright and anxiety. He found it difficult to perform in front of large crowds and often felt disconnected from his music. To cope with this, Einaudi began practicing mindfulness and meditation. He learned to focus on his breath and let go of his fears and anxieties.

Through his practice, Einaudi discovered the power of stillness and being present in the moment. He learned to connect more deeply with his music and his audience, and his performances became more confident and powerful as a result.

Today, Einaudi is considered one of the most successful and innovative composers of his generation. His music has been featured in films, television shows, and commercials, and he has won numerous awards and accolades for his work. Despite his success, Einaudi continues to prioritize mindfulness and presence in his life, recognizing the value of stillness and the power of music to connect us all.

"I care about decency and humanity and kindness. Kindness today is an act of rebellion." – Pink

Tony Hsieh

Tony Hsieh was known for his commitment to building a strong company culture that prioritized kindness, empathy, and customer service. He believed that treating employees well was not only the right thing to do, but also the key to long-term success.

One story that demonstrates Hsieh's commitment to kindness occurred in the early days of Zappos, when the company was struggling to make payroll. Hsieh personally loaned the company $100,000 to help it stay afloat. At the time, the company was not profitable and the loan was a significant risk for Hsieh.

However, Hsieh's investment paid off. Zappos eventually became a highly successful online shoe retailer and was sold to Amazon for $1.2 billion in 2009. When Zappos became profitable, Hsieh didn't ask for the loan to be repaid. Instead, he set up a program that would reward employees who demonstrated exceptional customer service with a portion of the loan.

The program was called "The Pipeline" and was designed to encourage employees to go above and beyond in their customer service duties. Each month, employees who received positive feedback from customers were entered into a drawing, with the winner receiving a portion of the $100,000 loan.

The Pipeline was just one example of how Tony Hsieh's belief in the power of kindness helped him build a successful company that valued decency and humanity. Zappos became known for its exceptional customer service and strong company culture, with Hsieh often citing kindness as a key ingredient in the company's success.

"Everyone has inside of him a piece of good news. The good news is that you don't know how great you can be! How much you can love! What you can accomplish! And what your potential is!" - Anne Frank

Folorunso Alakija

Born on July 15, 1951, in Ikorodu, a Lagos suburb in Nigeria, Folorunso Alakija was raised in a middle-class family and was the second of four siblings. Her father was a politician and the Chief of the Adeyemo Alakija family, one of the most prominent families in Nigeria.

After completing her primary education in Nigeria, Alakija traveled to the United Kingdom, where she studied fashion design at the Central School of Fashion in London. She then returned to Nigeria to launch her own fashion label, which quickly became a success.

In the 1980s, Alakija ventured into the oil industry and obtained an oil prospecting license from the Nigerian government, which was later converted into an oil mining lease. Her company, Famfa Oil, now holds a 60% stake in the offshore OML 127 oil field, one of the largest oil reserves in Nigeria.

Alakija's success in the oil industry has made her one of the richest women in Africa. In 2014, she was listed by Forbes as the richest woman in Nigeria and the second-richest woman in Africa, with an estimated net worth of $2.5 billion.

Despite her success, Alakija has remained committed to giving back to her community. She is a devoted philanthropist and has established the Rose of Sharon Foundation, which provides scholarships, financial assistance, and other support to widows and orphans in Nigeria. She has also donated generously to various other causes, including healthcare, education, and the arts.

In recognition of her philanthropic work and her contributions to the Nigerian economy, Alakija has received numerous honors and awards over the years. She was appointed as the Chancellor of Osun State University in Nigeria in 2015 and was also awarded an honorary doctorate degree from the University of Lagos in 2019.

Alakija's story is a powerful reminder that with hard work, determination, and a strong sense of purpose, anyone can achieve great things and make a positive impact on the world.

"We must let go of the life we have planned, so as to accept the one that is waiting for us." - Joseph Campbell

Coco Chanel

Born in 1883 in Saumur, France, Coco Chanel faced a challenging childhood, as her father left the family, and her mother passed away when she was only 12 years old. As a result, Chanel and her siblings were sent to an orphanage in Aubazine, where she learned to sew.

After leaving the orphanage, Chanel worked as a seamstress and a singer in bars and clubs in Moulins, France. She adopted the name "Coco" during this time, and it soon became her nickname.

Chanel's dreams of becoming a famous singer did not come to fruition, but she continued to work in the fashion industry, making hats and designing clothes for her friends. In 1910, she opened her first boutique in Paris, which later became the famous Chanel brand.

Chanel's designs were a departure from the frilly and elaborate fashions of the time, and instead emphasized simplicity, comfort, and functionality. Her clothing was designed to liberate women from the constraints of traditional fashion, and her signature pieces included the little black dress, the Chanel suit, and the quilted handbag.

Chanel's success in the fashion industry was due in part to her ability to let go of the life she had planned as a singer, and instead embrace the one that was waiting for her in fashion. She adapted to new opportunities and embraced change, ultimately becoming one of the most successful fashion designers of all time.

Chanel's life is a testament to the power of resilience, determination, and creativity, and her legacy continues to influence the fashion industry to this day.

"Wake up determined, go to bed satisfied." - Dwayne "The Rock" Johnson

Lazlo Hanyecz

Lazlo Hanyecz was born in Florida, USA, in 1979. He became interested in computers at a young age and taught himself how to code. He studied computer science at the University of Florida, but dropped out after a year to pursue a career as a software developer.

In the early days of Bitcoin, when the digital currency was still largely unknown, Lazlo became interested in the technology behind it. He saw the potential for a decentralized, peer-to-peer payment system that could disrupt the traditional banking industry.

In May 2010, Lazlo decided to make the first real-world Bitcoin transaction. He posted on a Bitcoin forum offering to pay 10,000 Bitcoins to anyone who would order him two pizzas. A user named "Jercos" took him up on the offer and ordered the pizzas from Papa John's.

At the time, the exchange rate for Bitcoins was very low, and 10,000 of them were worth only a few dollars. But as the value of Bitcoin skyrocketed over the years, Lazlo's transaction became famous as one of the earliest and most expensive uses of the digital currency.

But Lazlo's success is not just about his involvement in the early days of Bitcoin. He has been a prolific contributor to open-source software projects, and has spent countless hours working to improve the technology behind Bitcoin and other cryptocurrencies. He has been involved in various Bitcoin-related projects, including a mining pool and a payment processing system.

Lazlo, despite his success, maintains a humble and grounded demeanor. He still lives a simple life, and has said that he doesn't regret spending his Bitcoins on pizza, because at the time he didn't think they would ever be worth anything. He continues to work on various software projects and remains active in the Bitcoin community.

Lazlo's story is a reminder that success is not just about making a fortune, but also about working hard, pursuing your passions, and staying true to yourself. It's about waking up every day with a sense of purpose and determination, and going to bed each night with the satisfaction of knowing that you did your best.

"Nobody built like you, you design yourself." - Jay-Z

Melanie Perkins

Melanie Perkins co-founded Canva, an online graphic design tool, in 2012. While studying at the University of Western Australia, Perkins was teaching graphic design to students and was frustrated with the lack of user-friendly tools available. She realized that designing graphics was difficult for most people, so she wanted to make a tool that could be used by anyone.

Perkins partnered with her boyfriend, Cliff Obrecht, and together they raised $3 million in funding to launch Canva. However, their journey to success was not an easy one. They faced multiple rejections and setbacks along the way, with many investors being skeptical of their idea. Perkins and Obrecht had to work hard to convince people to believe in their vision.

Despite these challenges, Perkins persevered and continued to work on the product. She spent countless hours designing and testing the platform, ensuring that it was user-friendly and met the needs of a wide range of users. Canva quickly gained popularity, especially among small businesses, bloggers, and social media marketers.

Today, Canva is valued at over $15 billion and has over 60 million users worldwide. It has become an essential tool for many businesses and individuals who need to create high-quality graphics, such as social media posts, presentations, and marketing materials. Perkins' success is a testament to the fact that success is not always about having a pre-determined path or a perfect plan, but rather about identifying a problem and being resourceful enough to find a solution. Through hard work and perseverance, she was able to design a successful business for herself and prove that anything is possible with determination and a willingness to take risks.

"I tell myself, 'You've been through so much, you've endured so much, time will allow me to heal, and soon this will be just another memory that made me the strong woman, athlete, and mother I am today.'" - Serena Williams

Jon Oringer

Jon Oringer is an American entrepreneur and the founder of Shutterstock, a stock photography, video, and music website. Before starting Shutterstock, Jon worked as a programmer and photographer in New York City. As a photographer, he often struggled to find affordable, high-quality stock images that he could use in his own work.

In 2003, Jon decided to start Shutterstock as a side project to solve this problem. He began by taking his own photographs and building the website from scratch. He even sold some of his own images on the platform to help get things started. Initially, Jon worked alone, coding and designing the site, and photographing every image himself.

As the website grew in popularity, Jon realized he had a hit on his hands and decided to quit his job to focus on Shutterstock full-time. In the early days, Jon and his team worked tirelessly to build out the platform and acquire new users. They hustled, attending trade shows and meeting with potential clients to drum up business.

Their hard work paid off, and Shutterstock quickly became one of the leading stock photography websites in the world. Today, Shutterstock has over 1 billion images, videos, and music tracks available for license, and the company is publicly traded on the New York Stock Exchange. Jon's net worth is estimated at over $1 billion, making him one of the most successful self-made entrepreneurs in the tech industry.

Through his vision and hard work, Jon Oringer has revolutionized the stock photography industry and provided a valuable service to photographers, designers, and businesses all over the world. His story is a testament to the power of determination, ingenuity, and perseverance..

"Our lives are stories in which we write, direct and star in the leading role. Some chapters are happy while others bring lessons to learn, but we always have the power to be the heroes of our own adventures." - Joelle Speranza

Adele

Adele Laurie Blue Adkins, known professionally as Adele, was born on May 5, 1988, in Tottenham, London. She grew up in a working-class family and was raised by her mother after her father left when she was just 3 years old. Adele struggled with dyslexia and spent most of her childhood singing and performing in choirs.

When she was 14, Adele discovered the music of Ella Fitzgerald and became inspired to pursue a career in music. She began singing in local clubs and venues and eventually recorded a three-song demo that caught the attention of XL Recordings. In 2008, Adele released her debut album "19" which included the hit single "Chasing Pavements". The album was both a critical and commercial success, earning Adele a Grammy Award for Best New Artist in 2009.

Adele's second album, "21", was released in 2011 and quickly became a global sensation. The album was inspired by a tumultuous relationship that Adele had experienced and included hits such as "Rolling in the Deep" and "Someone Like You". The album sold over 30 million copies worldwide and earned Adele six Grammy Awards, including Album of the Year.

Despite the success of "21", Adele took a break from music in 2012 to focus on her personal life. She gave birth to a son, Angelo, in 2012 and took time off to raise him. In 2015, she returned with her third album "25", which included the hit single "Hello". The album was another commercial and critical success, earning Adele five more Grammy Awards.

Adele's career has been marked by her authenticity, emotional songwriting, and powerful voice. She has been open about her struggles with depression and anxiety and has used her music to connect with her fans on a deep level. Despite facing personal challenges, she has always remained in control of her own narrative and has continued to be the hero of her own adventure.

"Live your beliefs and you can turn the world around." - Henry David Thoreau

Mary Barra

Mary Barra is an American businesswoman who has been the CEO of General Motors since 2014. She started working for the company as a co-op student in 1980 while studying electrical engineering at Kettering University. After graduation, she joined GM full-time as an engineer and steadily climbed the corporate ladder, holding various roles in engineering, manufacturing, and human resources.

In 2013, Barra became the head of global product development at GM, where she oversaw the design, engineering, and quality of all GM vehicles worldwide. However, just a few months into her new role, she faced one of the biggest crises in the company's history.

It was discovered that some GM vehicles had a faulty ignition switch that could cause the engine to stall and disable the airbags, which had been linked to several deaths. Barra immediately took action, recalling millions of vehicles and setting up a victim compensation fund. She also conducted a thorough investigation to determine how the problem had gone undetected for so long, and she implemented new procedures to ensure that such a tragedy would never happen again.

Barra's leadership and transparency during the crisis earned her widespread praise. She appeared before Congress to testify about the recalls and faced tough questioning, but she remained calm and composed, emphasizing her commitment to fixing the problem and putting customers first.

Barra's actions during this crisis were in line with her personal beliefs and values, which include prioritizing safety, transparency, and accountability. She has often spoken about the importance of doing the right thing, even when it's difficult, and her actions during the recall crisis demonstrated this principle in action. As a result, Barra has become widely respected as a successful and ethical leader in the automotive industry, and she continues to push for innovation and sustainability in her role at GM.

"Don't try to lessen yourself for the world; let the world catch up to you." – Beyoncé

Sophia Amoruso

Sophia Amoruso's journey to success started when she was just 22 years old and was selling vintage clothing on eBay. She had a keen eye for fashion and a talent for marketing, and quickly built-up a following of customers who loved her unique and edgy style.

As her eBay business grew, Amoruso started to focus more on building her own brand. In 2006, she launched Nasty Gal Vintage, an online store that specialized in vintage clothing and accessories. The brand was an instant hit with young women who were looking for something different from the mainstream fashion world.

Amoruso's success didn't come without its challenges. She faced financial difficulties early on and had to work hard to keep her business afloat. She also had to navigate the ups and downs of running a rapidly growing company, including dealing with employees, suppliers, and investors.

Despite these challenges, Amoruso remained true to herself and her vision. She continued to push the boundaries of what was possible in the fashion world, creating bold and daring designs that were unlike anything else on the market.

In 2014, Amoruso wrote a book called #GIRLBOSS that became an instant bestseller. The book was a manifesto for young women who wanted to be their own bosses and achieve their dreams, and it was filled with practical advice and inspiring stories from Amoruso's own life.

While Nasty Gal ultimately faced some setbacks and Amoruso stepped down as CEO in 2015, her story remains a powerful reminder that it's possible to achieve great success by staying true to yourself and your vision, even when the odds are stacked against you.

"Faith is love taking the form of aspiration." - William Ellery Channing

Shahid Khan

Shahid Khan was born in Pakistan in 1950 and came to the United States in 1967 to study engineering at the University of Illinois. He worked part-time washing dishes while studying and graduated in 1971 with a degree in industrial engineering.

After graduation, Khan worked as a design engineer for a company in Illinois before he decided to start his own business in 1978. With a $16,000 loan and his engineering expertise, he founded Flex-N-Gate, a company that produced bumpers for pickup trucks. Over the years, Khan grew the business by expanding its product line and acquiring other companies.

Khan's faith has always played a central role in his life and his career. In an interview with CNN, he said, "I believe that my faith has helped me in every step of my life." He also spoke about how his faith gives him a sense of purpose and direction, and helps him navigate the challenges of business and life.

Khan's optimistic outlook and determination have also been key factors in his success. In an interview with Inc., he said, "I'm an optimist, and I believe that anything is possible. I'm also a realist, so I know that it takes hard work and dedication to achieve your goals."

Today, Khan is one of the most successful businessmen in the United States, with a net worth of over $8 billion. In addition to his work with Flex-N-Gate, he is also the owner of the NFL's Jacksonville Jaguars and the English Premier League's Fulham FC.

Shahid Khan's journey serves as a powerful example of how unwavering faith, tireless effort, and a relentless drive to succeed can pave the way to great accomplishments. His unwavering belief in himself and his ability to achieve his dreams is a true example of how "Faith is love taking the form of aspiration.".

"If you don't like the road you're walking, start paving another one!" - Dolly Parton

Tara Westover

Tara Westover's story is one of perseverance and self-discovery. She was raised in a strict, survivalist family in rural Idaho, where her parents rejected mainstream society and formal education. Westover did not attend school until she was 17 years old, and her education was limited to reading the Bible and working in her family's scrapyard.

Despite these obstacles, Westover was determined to learn more about the world beyond her isolated upbringing. She began to teach herself mathematics and grammar, and studied for the ACT exam in secret. When she earned a high score on the exam, she applied to Brigham Young University and won a full scholarship.

At university, Westover struggled to adjust to the demands of academic life and the social norms of mainstream society. She also had to confront the emotional and physical abuse that she had experienced at the hands of her family. Nevertheless, she persisted in her studies and went on to earn a Bachelor's degree in History and a Master's degree in Philosophy.

Westover's pursuit of education and personal growth continued after she left BYU. She won a Gates Cambridge Scholarship to study at Cambridge University, where she earned a PhD in History. Her research focused on the history of radicalism and violence in America, and she has written and spoken extensively on these topics.

In 2018, Westover published her memoir, "Educated", which became a bestseller and garnered critical acclaim. The book tells the story of her journey from an isolated, abusive upbringing to a life of intellectual and personal freedom. It has been praised for its raw honesty, insight into the power of education, and the resilience of the human spirit.

Overall, Tara Westover's story is a testament to the power of education, perseverance, and the human capacity for growth and self-discovery. She exemplifies the idea that if you don't like the road you're walking, you can chart a new path for yourself through determination, learning, and a willingness to embrace new experiences.

"When it comes to luck, you make your own." - Bruce Springsteen

Howard Schultz

Howard Schultz was born and raised in a housing complex for low-income families in Brooklyn, New York. He attended Northern Michigan University on a football scholarship and later went on to work for Xerox before joining Starbucks in 1982.

At the time, Starbucks was a small coffee bean roasting company with only four locations in Seattle. Schultz was tasked with marketing their products to businesses and consumers. In 1983, he went on a business trip to Milan, Italy, where he discovered the country's rich coffee culture and the potential for creating high-end coffee shops in the United States.

Schultz returned to Seattle and proposed the idea of opening a coffee shop that would serve as a "third place" between home and work, where people could come to relax and enjoy high-quality coffee. However, Starbucks' founders weren't interested in the idea, so Schultz left the company and started his own coffee shop called Il Giornale.

Within a few years, Il Giornale had grown to six locations, and Schultz saw an opportunity to purchase Starbucks and merge the two companies. He eventually acquired the company in 1987 and began to expand the Starbucks brand to new locations and products.

Schultz's success with Starbucks can be attributed to his passion for the product and his willingness to take a risk and pursue his vision, even when others didn't see the potential. While he was lucky to have discovered the Italian coffee culture, he made his own luck by acting on that inspiration and creating his own path. Today, Starbucks has over 31,000 locations worldwide and is one of the most successful coffee chains in the world.

"We generate fears while we sit. We overcome them by action." - Dr. Henry Link

Thomas Tull

Thomas Tull's story is one of perseverance, determination, and taking calculated risks. He was born in Endwell, New York, and grew up in a family of modest means. Tull was always interested in movies and filmmaking, but he didn't start pursuing his dream until he was in his thirties.

After college, Tull worked in finance and eventually became a successful investment manager. However, he never lost his passion for movies, and he began investing in independent films as a hobby. In 2003, Tull decided to take a risk and invest his own money in the production of Batman Begins, a reboot of the Batman film franchise directed by Christopher Nolan.

Tull knew that the film industry was notoriously difficult to break into, and he was afraid of failing. However, he believed in the project and was willing to take a chance. He invested over $10 million of his own money in the production of Batman Begins, which was a risky move at the time.

Despite his fears, Tull's investment paid off. Batman Begins was a critical and commercial success, grossing over $370 million at the box office worldwide. The success of the film launched Tull's career in the film industry and paved the way for the creation of Legendary Entertainment.

In 2005, Tull founded Legendary Entertainment with the goal of producing high-quality, blockbuster movies. Over the years, the company has produced many successful films, including The Dark Knight, Inception, Godzilla, and Jurassic World. Tull's willingness to take risks and overcome his fears through action has led to a successful career in the movie industry and serves as an inspiration for others to pursue their dreams despite any fears or obstacles that may arise.

"I have learned over the years that when one's mind is made up, this diminishes fear; knowing what must be done does away with fear." - Rosa Parks

Wendy Davis

Wendy Davis is a former Democratic state senator from Texas who gained national attention in 2013 for her efforts to block a bill that would have severely restricted access to abortion in Texas. Davis was initially thought to have little chance of stopping the bill, which was backed by a Republican-controlled legislature, but she refused to back down and decided to fight the bill with a filibuster.

In June 2013, Davis began an 11-hour filibuster on the floor of the Texas State Senate, speaking continuously to prevent the bill from being passed before the legislative session ended. Wearing pink sneakers and a back brace, Davis stood and spoke for over 11 hours, without taking a break or even leaning on her desk for support. She read personal stories from women who had experienced difficulty accessing reproductive healthcare and shared her own experience as a single mother who had faced similar challenges.

As the hours wore on, Davis faced intense opposition from Republicans who accused her of violating parliamentary rules and tried to shut her down. Despite these obstacles, Davis persisted, and her efforts inspired thousands of supporters who packed the state Capitol to witness the historic event.

Ultimately, Davis was successful in temporarily blocking the bill's passage, but it was eventually passed in a subsequent legislative session. However, Davis' filibuster had a significant impact on the reproductive rights movement and helped to energize supporters across the country. Her determination and courage in the face of opposition are a testament to the power of having a clear goal and the resolve to see it through, even in the face of fear and adversity.

"The moral of my story is the sun always comes out after the storm. Being optimistic and surrounding yourself with positive loving people is for me, living life on the sunny side of the street." - Janice Dean

Bethany Hamilton

Bethany Hamilton was born on February 8, 1990, in Lihue, Hawaii, and grew up in a family of surfers. She started surfing at a very young age and quickly showed a natural talent for the sport. At the age of 13, while surfing with her friend Alana Blanchard and her family, a 14-foot tiger shark attacked Bethany, biting off her left arm.

The attack was a traumatic and life-changing experience for Bethany, but she remained optimistic and determined to continue pursuing her passion for surfing. With the help of her family and friends, she underwent a rigorous rehabilitation program and worked hard to rebuild her strength and confidence.

Just three weeks after the attack, Bethany was back in the water, surfing with one arm. She quickly adapted to her new reality, using a specially designed board and learning new techniques to compensate for the loss of her arm.

Bethany's positive attitude and determination in continuing to compete in surf competitions despite the challenges she faced quickly made her an inspiration to others. In 2004, she won the

NSSA National Surfing Championship, becoming the first surfer to win a national title with only one arm.

Bethany's story gained international attention and she became a role model for people around the world, sharing her story and inspiring others to overcome their own challenges. She wrote a book about her experience, "Soul Surfer: A True Story of Faith, Family, and Fighting to Get Back on the Board," which was later turned into a movie in 2011.

Today, Bethany is still an active surfer and continues to compete in professional competitions. She is also a motivational speaker and advocates for various charitable causes. Her story is a powerful reminder that with a positive attitude and the support of loved ones, we can overcome even the most difficult challenges and achieve great things.

"Dreams don't have to just be dreams. You can make it a reality; if you just keep pushing and keep trying, then eventually you'll reach your goal. And if that takes a few years, then that's great, but if it takes 10 or 20, then that's part of the process." - Naomi Osaka

Nikola Tesla

Nikola Tesla was born in 1856 in Smiljan, Croatia. From a young age, he showed an exceptional aptitude for science and mathematics, and he began studying engineering in Austria in the 1870s. After completing his studies, Tesla worked for several years as an assistant to the famous inventor and electrical engineer Thomas Edison.

Tesla quickly became disillusioned with Edison's approach to electrical engineering, which relied heavily on direct current (DC) technology. Tesla believed that alternating current (AC) was a far superior system, as it allowed for more efficient transmission of electrical power over long distances.

After parting ways with Edison, Tesla set up his own laboratory and began developing his own AC electrical system. However, his efforts were met with resistance from many in the scientific community, who were skeptical of his ideas and wary of the potential dangers of high-voltage electricity.

Despite these setbacks, Tesla continued to work tirelessly in his laboratory, experimenting with new designs and technologies.

He was eventually able to convince investors to fund his work, and in 1891, he patented his first AC motor.

Over the next several years, Tesla continued to develop and refine his AC system, overcoming numerous obstacles and setbacks along the way. His breakthrough came in 1893, when he was commissioned to design the electrical system for the Chicago World's Columbian Exposition. Tesla's AC system was a resounding success, powering the entire exposition and proving the viability of AC technology on a large scale.

Tesla went on to develop numerous other inventions throughout his career, including the Tesla coil and wireless communication technology. However, his work on AC technology remained one of his most significant achievements, revolutionizing the way we generate and distribute electrical power.

Tesla remained persistent and committed to his vision of utilizing electricity for the betterment of humanity, despite enduring numerous obstacles and failures throughout his career. His persistence and determination ultimately paid off, and his legacy continues to inspire new generations of inventors and innovators.

"We are not our best intentions. We are what we do." – Amy Dickinson

Jeff Bezos

Jeff Bezos' "two pizza rule" was part of his philosophy of creating a lean and efficient company culture at Amazon. He believed that small teams were more effective and could move faster and be more innovative than larger teams. In the early days of Amazon, Bezos would often hold meetings with small teams and bring in only two pizzas, which was enough to feed everyone on the team.

However, as the company grew and expanded, the "two pizza rule" was sometimes ignored, and teams grew larger and less efficient. Bezos recognized that this was a problem, and he believed that it was important to maintain a culture of small, nimble teams in order to keep the company's edge.

In an email sent to the entire company, Bezos announced that the "two pizza rule" was to be reinstated immediately. He emphasized that this was not just a symbolic gesture, but a real commitment to efficiency and innovation. Bezos also explained that the two-pizza rule was a way to ensure that meetings remained productive, and that everyone on a team was able to contribute and be heard.

By reinforcing his commitment to this principle, Bezos demonstrated that he was not just a leader with good intentions, but someone who was willing to take action to ensure that those intentions were put into practice. This anecdote shows that it is not enough to simply have good intentions or beliefs, but that true success comes from putting those beliefs into action and being vigilant in upholding them, even in the face of growth and success.

"We've been making our own opportunities, and as you prove your worth and value to people, they can't put you in a box. You hustle it into happening, right?" - Jennifer Lopez

Jan Koum

Jan Koum's success story is an inspiring example of how perseverance and hard work can lead to great achievements. Koum was born in Kiev, Ukraine in 1976, and he immigrated to the United States with his mother in 1992 when he was just 16 years old. They settled in a small apartment in Mountain View, California, where they lived off food stamps and struggled to make ends meet.

Despite the challenges, Koum was determined to succeed. He enrolled at San Jose State University and began working as a cleaner in a grocery store to support himself and his mother. He eventually taught himself computer programming and landed a job at Yahoo in 1997, where he met Brian Acton.

Koum and Acton became good friends and worked together on several projects. In 2007, Koum bought an iPhone and was impressed by the App Store. He saw an opportunity to create a messaging app that was simple and easy to use, and he began working on the idea for WhatsApp in his spare time.

Koum and Acton officially launched WhatsApp in 2009. The app quickly gained popularity because it was fast, reliable, and easy to use. People all over the world started using it to stay in touch with their friends and family. Koum and Acton worked tirelessly to improve the app and add new features, and by 2014, WhatsApp had over 400 million users.

In February 2014, Facebook acquired WhatsApp for $19 billion, making Koum a billionaire. Today, WhatsApp has over 2 billion users worldwide, and it continues to be one of the most popular messaging apps in the world.

Koum's success is a testament to the idea that with hard work, determination, and a great idea, anyone can make their own opportunities and achieve great success. Despite the challenges he faced as an immigrant and a young entrepreneur, Koum never gave up on his dream, and his perseverance paid off in a big way.

"I believe that if you'll just stand up and go, life will open up for you. Something just motivates you to keep moving." - Tina Turner

Simon Cowell

Simon Cowell is a music executive and television personality from the UK who has had a highly successful career in the music and entertainment industry. Cowell's story is a great example of someone who has persevered through numerous setbacks and ultimately achieved great success by staying focused and dedicated to his passions.

Cowell was born in London in 1959 and attended school in the UK before dropping out at the age of 16. After leaving school, he worked a series of odd jobs before landing a position in the mailroom of a music publishing company. This experience gave him a taste of the music industry and inspired him to pursue a career in music.

Over the years, Cowell worked his way up through the ranks and eventually became a record producer and A&R executive. He worked with a variety of successful musicians and bands, including Sinitta, Westlife, and the Spice Girls, among others.

In the early 2000s, Cowell became a judge on the reality TV show "Pop Idol" (later known as "American Idol"), where he gained a reputation for his blunt critiques and high standards. He quickly became one of the most recognizable faces on television, known for his acerbic wit and no-nonsense approach to judging.

In addition to his work on "Pop Idol," Cowell went on to create and produce several successful music and talent shows, including "The X Factor," "Britain's Got Talent," and "America's Got Talent." These shows have helped launch the careers of many talented performers, and have cemented Cowell's status as a leading figure in the entertainment industry.

Throughout his career, Cowell has faced numerous challenges and criticisms. He has been accused of being too harsh on contestants, and has had to deal with the ups and downs of the music industry. However, he has always remained focused on his goals and has never let setbacks deter him from pursuing his passion for music and entertainment.

Today, Cowell is widely regarded as one of the most successful and influential figures in the music and television industries. His story is a testament to the power of perseverance and determination, and a great example of how staying focused and dedicated to one's passions can lead to great success.

"How wild it was, to let it be." - Cheryl Strayed

Tina Fey

Tina Fey is an American comedian, writer, actress, and producer, who has had a long and successful career in the entertainment industry. Fey first gained fame as a writer and cast member on the popular sketch comedy show "Saturday Night Live" (SNL) in the late 1990s and early 2000s. She went on to create and star in the acclaimed sitcom "30 Rock," and has also appeared in numerous films and TV shows.

However, Fey's path to success was not always easy. In the early days of her career, she worked as an improv comedian in Chicago, where she struggled to make a name for herself in the male-dominated world of comedy. She often found herself being overlooked or dismissed by her male colleagues, and it took her some time to find her comedic voice.

One night, Fey was performing in a show when she suddenly realized that the audience was really responding to her material. She later described the experience as feeling like "a wild animal let out of its cage." This moment of recognition gave Fey the confidence to continue honing her skills and pursuing her dreams.

Fey's hard work and determination eventually paid off, and she went on to become one of the most successful and influential comedians of her generation. Her work on SNL and "30 Rock" helped to redefine the genre of sketch comedy and made her a role model for aspiring comedians and writers, particularly women.

Fey has been a vocal advocate for women in the entertainment industry and has actively worked to increase opportunities for female comedians and writers throughout her career. She has been recognized for her contributions with numerous awards, including multiple Emmy Awards, Golden Globes, and Screen Actors Guild Awards. Today, she is widely regarded as one of the most talented and influential figures in comedy.

"You have to be where you are to get where you need to go." -Amy Poehler

Kevin O'Leary

Kevin O'Leary, who is best known for his role on the television show "Shark Tank," began his career as a television producer in Canada in the 1980s. As a young producer, O'Leary was tasked with menial jobs, such as fetching coffee and running errands for his boss.

O'Leary remained determined to make the most of his job, despite its unglamorous nature. He worked hard and used the opportunity to network and learn about the television industry.

During his time as a producer, O'Leary made connections with other producers, directors, and executives in the industry. He also gained valuable insights into the importance of marketing and branding, skills that would later become critical to his success as an entrepreneur.

O'Leary eventually left the television industry to start his own software company. He used the connections and knowledge he had gained during his time as a producer to build his business and market his products effectively.

In one interview, O'Leary said that he learned a valuable lesson during his early days as a producer: "You have to be where you are to get where you need to go." He explained that this lesson helped him to stay focused on his current situation and make the most of the opportunities that were available to him at the time.

O'Leary's success as an entrepreneur and investor can be traced back to his willingness to learn and make the most of his position, even when it wasn't glamorous or exciting. This anecdote highlights the importance of being present in the moment and using your current situation as a learning opportunity, rather than always focusing on the next big thing

"You do not find the happy life. You make it." - Camilla Eyring Kimball

Lesley Stahl

Lesley Stahl's journey to finding happiness was not an easy one. As a successful journalist and correspondent for CBS's "60 Minutes," she was used to the fast-paced, high-stress world of news reporting. However, when her husband was diagnosed with multiple sclerosis, everything changed.

At first, Stahl found it difficult to balance her demanding career with caring for her husband and family. She struggled with feelings of guilt and uncertainty, and worried that she was neglecting the people she loved most.

However, over time, Stahl began to realize that she needed to make a change. She decided to step back from her work at "60 Minutes" and take a more active role in caring for her husband and family. She also started to explore new hobbies and interests, and found new meaning in helping others.

One of the most significant changes in Stahl's life came when she became a grandmother. She found that caring for her grandchildren brought her an incredible sense of joy and fulfillment, and helped her see the world in a new light.

Stahl has since returned to her work as a journalist, but with a newfound sense of purpose and perspective. She has continued to prioritize her family and personal life, and has written about her experiences in her book "Becoming Grandma."

Through her journey, Stahl has demonstrated that happiness is not something that can be found by chance, but rather something that must be actively pursued and created. By taking control of her life and prioritizing the things that truly matter to her, she has been able to find a sense of joy and fulfillment that she never thought possible.

"Definitions belong to the definers, not the defined."
— Toni Morrison

Viola Davis

Viola Davis is a highly accomplished actress known for her stunning performances on stage and screen. She is the first Black woman to achieve the "Triple Crown of Acting," which includes winning an Emmy, Tony, and Oscar award for acting. However, Davis's path to success was not easy, and she had to overcome significant obstacles to achieve her goals.

In interviews, Davis has spoken candidly about the limited roles available to Black actresses in Hollywood. She has discussed the frustration of being typecast in stereotypical roles, such as the sassy best friend or the angry Black woman. Davis has also discussed the pressure to conform to Hollywood's narrow definitions of beauty and success, which often exclude people of color.

Davis did not allow the challenges to define her or set limitations on her capabilities. She knew that she had the talent and the drive to succeed, and she was determined to find roles that showcased her abilities as an actress. Rather than settling for stereotypical roles, Davis sought out characters with depth and complexity, such as the troubled mother in the movie "Doubt" and the hard-working maid in "The Help."

Davis' hard work and determination have earned her a well-deserved reputation as one of the most respected actresses in Hollywood. She has won critical acclaim and numerous awards for her performances, and she has inspired a generation of Black actresses to pursue their dreams.

Davis's story is a powerful reminder that we should not let others define us and that success is not based on external definitions or stereotypes, but rather on our own hard work and determination. It illustrates the idea that "Definitions belong to the definers, not the defined." Davis refused to be defined by Hollywood's narrow expectations of what a Black actress should be, and she redefined success on her own terms. By doing so, she was able to achieve incredible success and inspire others to do the same.

"Whatever you think the world is withholding from you, you are withholding from the world." - Eckhart Tolle

Angie Hicks

Angie Hicks was a recent college graduate living in Columbus, Ohio in the early 1990s. She and her husband were renovating their home, but they struggled to find reliable and trustworthy contractors to help with the job. They were frustrated by the lack of information available to homeowners about the quality of local service providers, and Angie felt like the world was withholding good, honest contractors from her.

Angie initially tried to solve the problem by creating a referral service for homeowners. She contacted contractors and asked them to pay a fee to be included on her list of recommended providers. However, this approach didn't work because contractors weren't interested in paying for referrals.

Undeterred, Angie decided to take a different approach. She realized that the best way to help homeowners find reliable contractors was to provide them with reviews and ratings from other homeowners. In 1995, she founded Angie's List, a website that allowed homeowners to rate and review local service providers. The website was initially focused on home improvement, but it later expanded to include a variety of services, from healthcare to automotive repair.

Angie's List was an immediate hit with homeowners who were frustrated by the lack of reliable information about local service providers. The website grew rapidly, and Angie soon found herself running a successful business. She became the face of Angie's List, appearing in commercials and speaking at events to promote the website.

Currently, Angie's List is a publicly traded corporation with a market capitalization exceeding $500 million. The website has millions of members who use it to find reliable service providers in their area. Angie Hicks is still involved with the company as a board member, but she has also used her success to support other entrepreneurs. She serves on the board of several non-profit organizations that help entrepreneurs and small business owners, and she is a sought-after speaker on entrepreneurship and innovation.

"You must find the place inside yourself where nothing is impossible." - Deepak Chopra

Beth Comstock

Beth Comstock is a former Vice Chair of General Electric (GE) and a champion of innovation and entrepreneurship. She began her career as a journalist and later transitioned into corporate communications, working for NBC, CBS, and Turner Broadcasting. She joined GE in 1986 as Chief Marketing Officer of NBC, which at the time was owned by GE.

Comstock quickly distinguished herself at GE, holding a series of high-level leadership roles, including President of Integrated Media at NBC Universal and Chief Marketing Officer of GE. Throughout her tenure, she played a critical role in shaping the company's direction and driving innovation, particularly around digital transformation and new business creation.

One of Comstock's most significant contributions was the creation of GE Ventures, a venture capital subsidiary that invested in startups focused on energy, healthcare, and transportation. Under her leadership, GE Ventures invested in more than 100 companies, generating significant returns for the company.

Despite her many successes, Comstock faced a number of challenges throughout her career, including self-doubt and imposter syndrome. In an interview with Harvard Business Review, she recalled struggling with her identity as a woman in a male-dominated industry, as well as the fear of failure and the pressure to conform.

Despite these challenges, Comstock refused to be deterred. She worked hard to cultivate a mindset of resilience and perseverance, believing that anything was possible if she stayed true to her vision and remained committed to her goals.

Comstock is now highly regarded as a pioneer in the fields of innovation and entrepreneurship. She serves on the board of directors for Nike and recently published a memoir, "Imagine It Forward," in which she shares her insights on leadership, innovation, and personal growth. Comstock's story serves as a powerful reminder that with the right mindset and a commitment to excellence, anyone can achieve success and make a difference in the world.

Thinking Outside the Box: How a Shift in Perspective Can Drive Motivation and Innovation

As a writer who has spent decades exploring the intricacies of human motivation and innovation, I've come to believe that the key to unlocking these elusive qualities lies in reversing our perspective. By looking at things from a new angle, we can gain fresh insights that enable us to break free from old habits and embrace new, more creative approaches to problem-solving.

One of the most important things we can do to tap into our innate motivation is to stop relying on external rewards or punishments to drive us forward. Instead, we need to cultivate an internal sense of purpose and passion that comes from within. This means digging deep to uncover our core values and desires, and then aligning our actions with these fundamental principles. When we operate from a place of authenticity and integrity, we're much more likely to find the inspiration and energy we need to tackle even the most challenging tasks.

Another key element of motivation is the ability to stay curious and open-minded, even in the face of uncertainty or failure. Rather than viewing setbacks as signs of our inadequacy, we need to embrace them as opportunities for growth and learning. By experimenting with new approaches and perspectives, we can expand our horizons and discover new solutions to old problems.

Innovation, too, often springs from a willingness to see things in a new light. By stepping outside of our comfort zones and exploring uncharted territory, we can tap into our creativity and discover new ways of doing things. This may involve breaking

163

free from old patterns and routines, challenging conventional wisdom, and taking risks that others might shy away from.

At the same time, innovation also requires a deep understanding of the needs and desires of our fellow human beings. By empathizing with others and tuning into their perspectives, we can gain valuable insights that help us create products, services, and experiences that truly resonate with them. Whether we're working in business, education, or any other field, the ability to connect with others on a human level is essential to fostering innovation and driving positive change.

Of course, none of this is easy. It takes courage, persistence, and a willingness to embrace discomfort and uncertainty. But the rewards are immense. By tapping into our innate motivation and exploring new perspectives on innovation, we can transform our lives, our communities, and our world. So let's start today, by taking small steps towards our goals, embracing failure as a natural part of the process, and staying open to the unexpected opportunities that life presents us with. Together, we can create a future that is brighter, more innovative, and more full of possibilities than we ever imagined.

Printed in Great Britain
by Amazon